Praise for SPIN CONTROL

"This is a must read for every American who has gotten tired of the way things have become in politics and the news."
David Talbot, SALON.COM

"SPIN CONTROL will serve as a wake-up call for the reporting profession. Very insightful, sharp, cutting and funny."
Lara Spencer, ABC-TV

"This book should serve as a textbook for any student in college who wants to be a reporter. SPIN CONTROL is a no-holds-barred read that leaves no stone unturned in what's wrong with today's politcal world."
Nancy Ruhling, NEWSDAY

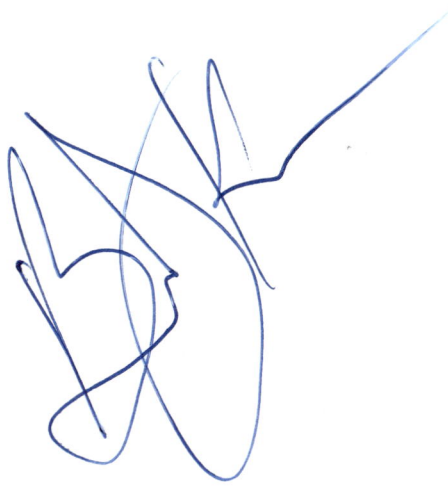

Also by Brian J. Karem

Shield the Source
(New Horizon Press, 1992)

Above the Law
(Pinnacle Books, 1999)

Innocent Victims
(Pinnacle Books, 2000)

Spin Control
essays and short stories

by
Brian J. Karem

BROOKEVILLE PRESS

Copyright © 2000 by Brian J. Karem

ISBN 0-9676516-1-1

All rights reserved. No part of this book may be reproduced or transmitted in any form or in any means, electronic or mechanical, including photocopying, recording or by any information and retrieval system without prior written permission from the publisher.

The Politics of Truth appeared in *San Antonio* September, 1989.
One Local Reporter's Tale of War first appeared in Electronic Media, April 22, 1991.
Yo, Media This! and *Oh God!* first appeared in the *San Antonio Current* March 18, 1993.
Reprinted by permission.

Prejudices, Sixth Series by H. L. Mencken. Copyright © 1927 by Alfred A. Knopf, Inc. and renewed 1955 by H. L. Mencken. Reprinted by permission of Alfred A. Knopf, Inc., a Division of Random House, Inc.

Brookeville Press
18825 Aplenglow Ln.
Brookeville, MD 20833-2705

Visit our website at brookevillepress.com

Cover photo by P. J. Russell
Back cover photos courtesy of author's collection.
Cover design by Alton Creative.   www.altoncreative.com.

Printed in the United States of America.

Spin Control
essays and short stories

by
Brian J. Karem

Table of Contents

Acknowledgements
Introduction

Essays

Naïvely Clinging to Hope	23
American Journalism in the 21st Century	33
Of Politicians and the Press	47
Speaking of the Truth	53
The Politics of Truth	59
One Local Reporter's Tale of War	69
Yo, Media This!	77
Oh God!	83
The Ties That Divide	89
My, My, But You Have a Fine	103
Dead Bodies and Pancake Makeup	117
Okay, Okay, the Real Story Is	133
Bozo's Got a Gun	143
Ode to Gordon Liddy	161

Short Stories

White Room	167
Tight Shoes	173
Spin Control	211
Another Reason Not to Eat Spaghetti	225
The Wet Spot	241
Free Flight	247
The Hummer	261
Just Before the Five Families War	267
That's Harry, Son	275
Who Forgot to Duck	281

For the three best people God ever put on earth:
Zachary, Brennan, and Wyatt

Acknowledgements

THERE ARE MANY I SHOULD acknowledge as being silent collaborators in this work, because without them I wouldn't have had the experience needed to write it. I may not have always agreed with everything these folks did nor will they uniformly agree that I was the easiest person to get along with when I worked with them. But, it was their decisions, their opinions, their sweat, and their interaction with me that helped me become who I am. Ultimately, if I'm happy with myself, how can I be upset with those who helped me become the person I stare at in the mirror every morning? I can't. So, I'd like to thank the many people who've helped guide me, argue with me, supervise me, and worked with me as comrades during my years as a reporter. They include, but aren't limited to, Barbara Fredrickson, Larry Bowen and Diane Bowen at the *Conroe Courier* in Conroe, Texas. Larry gave me my first big break in reporting. Mark Smith, one of my best friends from the old *Laredo News* as well as Peter Lee, our editor. Barry Bingham Sr. and everyone at the *Courier Journal* during the last great days of that newspaper before it sold out to Gannett. Dave Lander and Ken Kurtz at WKYT-TV. Everyone who ever worked in politics in either Texas, Missouri, or Kentucky. Ron Harig, Bob Donohue, and Forrest Carr at KMOL-TV, as well as Jeanne Jakle, the world's best, and, at the same time, most irritating newspaper television columnist. John Walsh, Lance and Vance Heflin, and everyone at *America's Most Wanted*. And among the others, Sam Donaldson, James Carville, and Steve Weinberg with IRE. Also, I want to thank my parents and give special thanks to Stan Knott in Kansas City.

And finally, thank you to my wife of the last 18 years, Pamela J.

Russell. She is not only physically attractive, but has the most attractive soul of anyone I've ever met. She must be a saint to stay with me all these years, to which everyone who knows me will uniformly admit.

Introduction

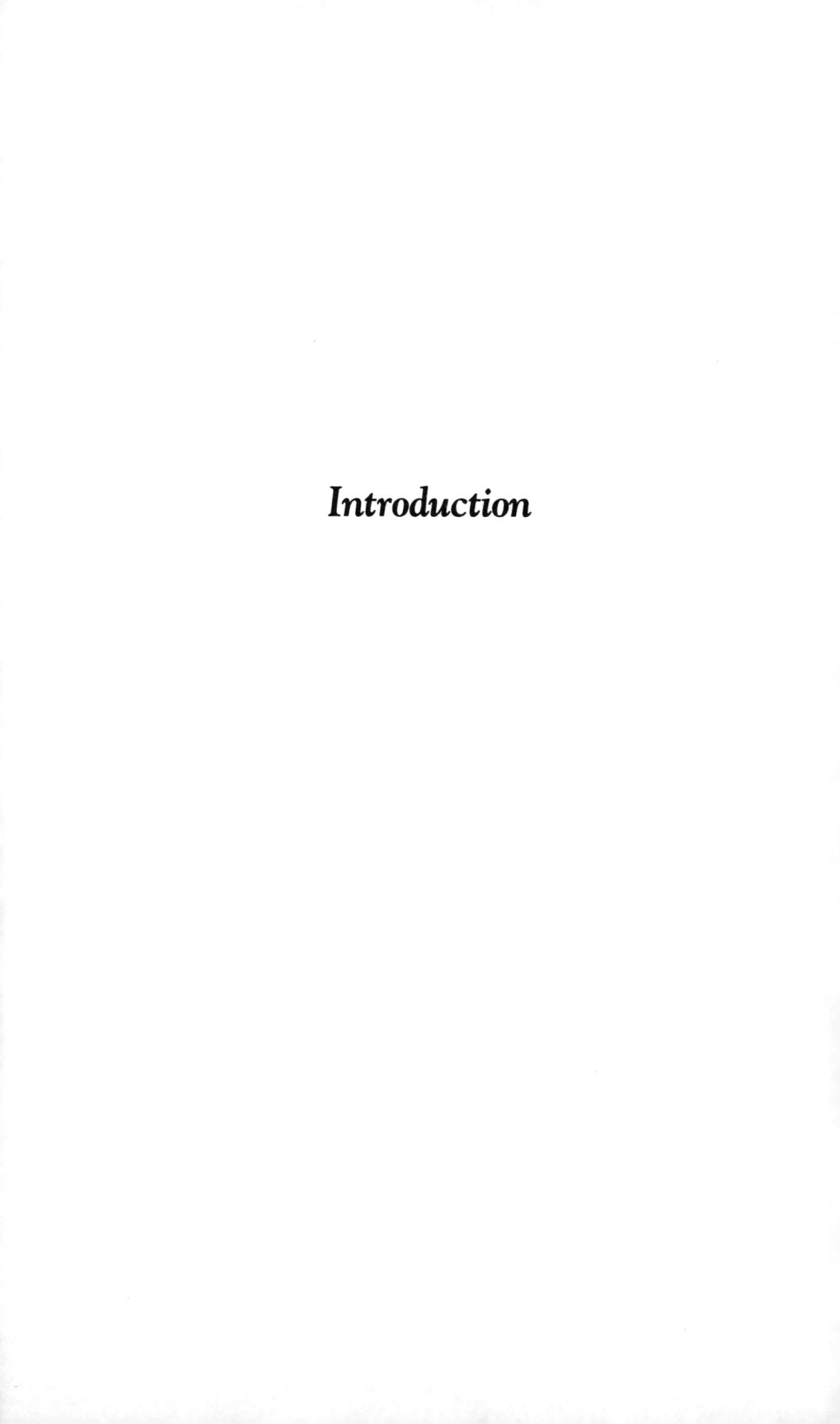

I HAVE BEEN ON A JOURNEY the last 25 years, and it has been a splendid journey. I cannot complain. I wanted to be a reporter. I wanted to travel the globe and cover important stories, and I wanted to inform my fellow citizens from a first-hand perspective.

I wanted to do this, and armed with the zeal of naïveté, youth, and moral conviction, I set out to commit Journalism with a capital "J".

I did not always succeed, and God, and some part of the population, was aware when I made mistakes. But, I'm human, and God also knows I made my mistakes while trying to err on the side of what I thought was right. So much for that.

Now, I believe the journey is over, or at least taking a different turn. I no longer wish to be a daily reporter, and it's not because of the intense deadlines, the travel nor the pressure of being first with a story. It's because of my children. Naïve again, perhaps, but there it is.

This need to change came over me slowly, and looking back on it, it becomes clear to me that it began when my father was diagnosed with lung cancer more than six-and-a-half years ago. They gave him about three months to live, and he stretched it out to two years, fighting the whole time against the odds and trying to cherish the moments he had left. He was very upset that he didn't spend more time with me when I was a child, but I told him it was okay. It was okay, for my childhood was over, and my father and I had spent a lot of time together since I had attained adulthood. But, I have to admit, part of me longed for the missed opportunities of being with my father when I was a child. I'm not alone in this, of course. I have many friends, several of whom are reporters, and one whose father is a national correspondent with a major network who regularly voiced the same opinions. They wished they'd had more time with their father.

I couldn't do anything about my lost time with my own father, but I began to want to spend more time with my own three sons so they wouldn't feel that same sense of loss when they were older. What cemented this was when my middle son, Brennan, was diagnosed with trichotrillo-mania. I had no idea what it was, but knew that any type of condition ending in "mania" wasn't good. As it turns out, it is compulsive hair pulling and is an anxiety-related condition brought on by various reasons, which probably included the fact that I was moving the family all over the country in pursuit of the "perfect" job.

That was when I decided to leave the daily grind. Now, I cover the stories I want, and I also get the opportunity on most days to walk my children to the bus stop, take care of them when they are sick or injured, and make damn sure they clean their rooms up and wear clean clothes and a belt- despite whatever the popular dress code of the day dictates.

It has meant a loss of revenue, a certain loss of stature- after all I'm no longer on the front lines, but as John Lennon once said, "I'm just sitting here watchin' the wheels go round and round. I really love to watch them roll."

Now, I write books, articles, and teach Sunday School to teenagers. I also speak at colleges and universities and at other venues about my experiences as a reporter. It is these appearances which have led me to write this book. During my time as a reporter, I felt we often did things wrong in the field and in how we put our newspapers and television broadcasts together. I've never been timid about voicing my concerns, but I've come to learn that the only people hearing me were those working in my field. Others need to hear.

I believe we cover race problems in this country in a horribly unjust and unenlightened manner. Hispanic reporters cover Hispanic events. Black reporters cover black events. This panders to the notion of political correctness while short-sightedly forgetting that this may not be the best way to report a story. For, I believe the real division in this country is not now and may never have been along racial or ethnic lines. I believe there is a class war going on in this country. I believe it began with Ronald Reagan and the "Me" Generation when it suddenly became popular and morally superior to be possessed of huge and ample portions of Greed.

Racial tensions have been very real and very disheartening, but the shame of it all is that we cannot understand that racial tension is merely a symptom of a class struggle. I may be skewered for saying it, but the O.J. Simpson case proved to me that at certain levels in this country, there is no such thing as racial discrimination. If you have money, you have no problems. You can buy your way out of anything. Money is the great leveler. All are equal under the dollar sign.

Many politicians know this, and yet do not act on it. Some of them have the best intentions, but are ultimately corrupted by the power of the dollar. They need it. They have to have it to get elected. And to be heard in the media, they have to pander to the lowest common denominator as much as television news does.

Speaking before college students, parents, and teens, I've also come to realize there is a certain naïveté to living in this country. We all simply try to take in the news we want to hear and dismiss the rest. We suffer from information overload and have a hard time filtering out the nonsense, so consequently some needed information is often left out of the mix. This came home to roost with me when my wife and I attended a neighborhood party. At the time, I was working for *America's Most Wanted*. I'd covered crime for years, and, as a consequence, I was very protective of my children. I wouldn't let them ride their bicycle out of view of the house. I was intimately knowledgeable of something called "Stranger Danger." If you've ever spoken at any length of time with John Walsh, his wife, or any parent who has lost a child, you know of what I speak. A moment can mean a lifetime lost. And there is nothing more painful than looking into the eyes of a parent who has lost a child. I cannot even describe it.

So, when I see parents, as I saw at this neighborhood barbecue, allowing their children to ride off to a friend's house on their bicycle a mile away from home, I couldn't help but want to explain to them why I'm a little more strict with my children. I don't judge them for their actions, but I do want them to know what they face as parents. Knowledge is a useful thing.

At the heart of this book, I hope you find that I deeply love my craft. I believe in the power of words and pictures. I believe in the democratic process and the system in this country. But, like the parents who weren't aware of "Stranger Danger," we are all a little less strident than we should be about the wonderful institutions in this country. We need to pay more attention, and we all need to be more actively involved. Hopefully, this book will show you why.

Finally, I've had this idea for a couple of years to put this book together. But, I hadn't settled on a venue nor had I approached a publisher via my very talented agent Peter Miller. Then I met Matthew Mullally. Matt's a young guy trying to put together a publishing company that will attract independent voices. I've always fancied myself an advocate of that type of thing, and inspired by Matt's energy and his commitment, I decided to give him this offering in support.

With that all said, I hope you enjoy the offering.

Brian J. Karem
4-2-00

Essays

Naïvely Clinging to Hope

I WOKE UP THIS MORNING slightly intimidated. The news was very disheartening. There are roughly twice as many people on earth today as on the day I was born. Naturally getting to know everyone on a first name basis is going to be next to impossible. It's one of my lifetime goals I guess I will have to abandon. Of course, the fact that we've managed to double our numbers in a little less than 40 years also is quite amazing considering AIDS, cancer, heart disease, war, and various Fox Television specials like *When Good Pets Go Bad* and *Who Wants to Marry a Multimillionaire?*

Even more amazing is the fact that we've been able to stretch the limited resources of this planet to feed a good many of these new residents. Farm production in the United States has indeed increased during the last 40 years while the total number of acres available for farming has decreased due to urban sprawl, highway construction, and the obsessive desire to turn your neighborhood supermarket into the one-stop shopping center from cradle to grave. Who, seriously, needs to be able to buy tires for your 1987 Honda Civic one aisle over from the frozen food section? Or better yet, when a recent study concluded that American children spend more time at the mall than doing their homework, why didn't anyone factor in the sheer size of these shopping behemoths as a reason for the discrepancy? It takes no rocket scientist to figure out that negotiating your way in and out of a mall- which sometimes is spread out over two zip codes- can cause serious damage to your schedule.

It is, of course, a side-effect to the burgeoning population, and it is evident everywhere as we plow down rain forests, dig up, fill in, and overrun the countryside in our vain attempts to homogenize and civilize all four corners of the globe. In this zeal to expand, there seems to be very little thought to what our children and grandchildren will be faced with in the future as we decimate every square inch of land in our attempt to provide housing, shopping and cyber-cafes for the expanding population. Indeed, there seems to be no thought about the future at all – just the desire to build and the need to provide more and more of what we have no idea until we're told what the hot new trend is by *Newsweek*, *Time*, and a host of other corporate magazines. Lest this sound like the rambling of an aging tree-hugger, let me confess right away that I subscribe to *Time* and *Newsweek* and have written for *People* and *Playboy* magazines. I am a true believer in the economic right to make as much money as Greed will allow and spend it lavishly on tennis shoes that are called "cross-trainers," tooth brushes that offer bent stems and the ability with their new bristles to scrub my lungs with one deep motion, and above all, being able to spoil my children with every gadget and article of clothing ill-conceived by the mind of man, including the all-pervasive need to spend unlimited funds on my children's shallow desire to own every Pokémon card in existence.

But has anyone thought, truly thought, about what happens in the future? I'm not talking about economic collapse, nuclear conflagration, the melting of the polar ice caps, nor of the disappearing ozone layer- although someone should probably be paying a little more attention to all of those cataclysmic changes as well. As John Lennon said, "Life is what happens to you while you're busy making other plans." So, while the world is planning on fighting, selling, praying, partying, reading, bending over, ripping someone off, whoring, sleeping, spending five dollars on a toothbrush, walking in the rain, burning Barry Manilow records, putting on pointy-headed bed sheets in the name of racial purity, preaching love, preaching hate, preaching spirituality, and day-trading online, the thing we seem to be doing best is doing as the Good Book says and being fruitful and multiplying. Where, in the next 30 or 40 years, do we intend to put all of these billions of new people? I've got space at my house for about two, so obviously we're all going to have to double up on our sleeping arrangements. Still, I suspect that won't solve the problem. My mother, for example, won't put anyone up at her place even if she has the room - she is such a neat freak she can't stand anyone messing up her place. This causes no end to problems when my wife and our three children visit for the holidays. So, I'm reasonably sure complete strangers don't stand a chance with her. I suspect there are many more like my mother out there. You've seen them. They are the people who vacuum their living rooms when they want to relax, pull out a 50-gallon barrel of weed killer to zap one stray dandelion in their lawn, and spend 30 minutes in front of the makeup mirror every morning gagging as they brush their tongue.

The question remains: what do we do with all of these people that are coming? Condoms, planned parenthood, and the desires of the state aside, there seems to be no stopping the coming population explosion. People just enjoy unprotected sex too damn much. It's cheap, it's easy, and thanks to prime time television, HBO, and the Internet, just about anyone can do it. Rumors are the Catholic Church used to have a patent on the process simply for procreation purposes, but the information age has brought the monopoly to a devastating end.

We are therefore left with a huge procreative force that is threatening to overrun the planet, much like unchecked bacteria in a test tube. And we all should know what happens when the bacteria population reaches a certain point. The bacteria use all of their resources in the test tube and then begin dying off, unable to sustain themselves. Will the same thing happen to the human race? Is AIDS, the Plague, heart disease, cancer, and a host of other diseases and conditions simply nature's way of playing Scrooge and killing off the surplus population?

More importantly, is the human race the multi-cellular equivalent of simple bacteria? Can we not control our destiny any better? Fortunately, all of these questions have been answered in the upcoming book, *Die You Zayon Pig*, by Dr. Leonard McCoy, who proposes that everyone simply masturbate twice a day, thereby eliminating the need to procreate. While a noble concept, I doubt it will enjoy much success. Generations of parents telling their children to "stop it or you will go blind," coupled with the old stand-by, "you'll grow hair on your palms," will, I surmise, be much too much to overcome, and the procreative arts will continue to flourish.

Which leaves us back at the fundamental problem of not enough space and too many people in the coming future. It is inevitable, and there will have to be many hard decisions made, if not by us, then by our children. In as much as our parents handed us this problem, perhaps without knowing it was a problem themselves, this does not give us the right to hand the problem down to our children. Let's face it. World War I and World War II, which gave rise to the existential movement among other absurdities, also brought to our parents the overwhelming notion that overpopulation would never be a big problem because we could be relatively assured that every 25 years or so the world would kill off as many people as possible in a massive display of genocide, violent war, and bad war slogans. Alas, nothing in this world is assured, so here we are.

After much humor, vacillation, and ignorance, there really is only one solution to the problem; we must leave the nest. Yes, yes, I know that sounds again like some New Age philosopher who wants to shed the vessel and head for the mothership behind the comet, but it isn't. Space travel has captured the nation's attention and imagination ever since John Kennedy challenged the nation to get to the Moon and return safely in perhaps the most tumultuous decade in the 20th Century. We did, too, and pinned to the wall in my home office is a constant reminder as to why I am no longer enthusiastic about American presidential politics.

It is a piece of needle-point that I crafted for a third grade project. Our teacher at the time, Mrs. Blount, thought it would be good if boys and girls learned a little about stitches. Perhaps she thought we would all become doctors or needlepoint artists. Who knows? But she did teach us a few stitches and then gave us some wildly colored yarn, a light bluish-green piece of what looked like burlap, and then turned us loose.

I remember getting a "B" on the project and was admonished for rushing through the effort. But I couldn't help myself. I'm sure Mrs. Blount, with her astute knowledge of obscure stitching patterns, wanted us to come up with something beautiful and amazing in our effort. Indeed, some children tried to stitch a swan, a mountain range, a dog, or a bird or something equally beautiful inspired by the artist and poet in all of us. I wasn't so inspired. For the only thing that I could think about in the fall of 1969 was NASA. I was too young to worry about the wrong colored acid at Woodstock, John McCain's "Gooks" in Vietnam or Richard Nixon's Dirty Tricks Club Band. In fact, nothing much of the outside world seemed to penetrate the smell of school paste and games like kick ball that seemed so imminently important to me and most of us at Goldsmith Elementary School in Louisville, Kentucky.

The one single exception was NASA. Neil Armstrong. Buzz Aldrin. Michael Collins. Apollo 11. The Eagle has landed. Columbia was in orbit. I and most of my friends had been enamored of the Space Program and NASA since we had been able to breathe. I collected every stray clipping from the newspaper that I could, back to late Mercury and early Gemini missions. Some of my earliest memories were of shut downs on the launch pad, docking with the Agena rocket, space walks, and the untimely launch pad fire and loss of my favorite astronaut, Gus Grissom, along with Roger Chaffee and Ed White. With blue construction paper, I had fashioned several files into which I dropped all of the articles I found on NASA's space flights. I even had allocated flight numbers and affixed the official flight insignia to each file I created and put them all together in one large binder. It was all about the romance, as I saw it, of Space Travel and the hope it gave me for our future. It was a future where people lived on the moon, colonized Mars and traveled to the stars. It was a future where you didn't have to worry about a stray asteroid wiping out the entire human race, for there would always be more than one rock in the solar system where people could and would live. NASA gave me dreams that I had never fathomed before or since.

Which brings me back to the needle-point project. Mine depicted the Apollo Command module separating from the Service Module for re-entry after a moon flight. Mrs. Blount, upon receiving it from me, asked if I knew who had gotten the space program started. I admitted I did not and that's when she told me my father's hero, John F. Kennedy, the first Catholic president, had challenged the nation to get to the moon before the end of the decade, and we had done it.

I marveled then and now at the fact that words could be used to move people so forcefully and along such monumentally noble paths. I don't think it's an overstatement to say the best and most impressive thing Kennedy did for this country and the world was to give birth to the Space Program and its byproducts, which include computers and the Internet Revolution. There really hasn't been anyone since Kennedy that could move a crowd the way he did and I haven't witnessed, since his time, a politician that could unite as he could. I never saw my father once cry for any man, let alone a politician, the way he cried when Kennedy died. I became proud of politicians because of Kennedy and that pride grew as I realized my grandfather and an uncle were circuit court judges while my other uncle was a state senator. And as I watched launch after launch of Mercury, Gemini and Apollo spacecraft on television- and collected my newspaper clippings- I became inspired not only by the politicians, but by the press which reported on everything about NASA and kept me informed via Walter Cronkite's ringside seat to history.

But over the years, I lost my files of newspaper articles and forgot the naïve enthusiasm I held in my childhood. The nation too seems to have forgotten its own past. Who could conceive of a politician in this day and age inspiring anyone the way Kennedy did? Reporters of the caliber of Geraldo Rivera have replaced the trusted Walter Cronkite. On the whole, politicians and the press alike seem to be nothing more than sideshow barkers hawking cheap remedies and snake oil as salves for our jaded American psyche.

Looking at the needle-point that served as a symbol of my inspiration as a child, I wonder who will inspire us now. I look at my own sons and wonder if there are any leaders, journalists, or noble causes like the Space Race left for them. Our race with the Soviet Union to get a man on the moon was choreographed by a generation whose ingenuity had already been tested and tempered by the suffering of a depression and the fires of the worst war ever waged on the planet.

The world is now run by us, the sons and daughters of that generation: the baby boomers. We have met the enemy and they are us, to paraphrase Pogo. Our parents, never wanting us to suffer as they did, gave us a world where the possibilities are limitless, and we waste our time with diversions derived from the ancillary technology that took us to the moon - Play Stations and computer games. Yet, as I look at that needle point on my wall, I still from time to time naïvely hold out the hope that we will one day find a politician who inspires rather than detracts. I look forward to someone who will share a vision and challenge us to reach it. Then I turn around at my neighbors and look myself in the mirror and realize that it must come from within us now.

I naïvely cling to the hope that in my lifetime I can visit the moon, that politicians will spend less time talking about stained dresses and more time talking and doing something about education and poverty, and I pray every night that the profession that I joined some 20 years ago will rebound from the carnival sideshow antics now rampant in the industry and provide people with useful and incisive information.

I continue to hope all of this, because if the statisticians are right, the world population is going to double again within my lifetime, and I believe the only hope for the human race is to expand off of this one globe to the Moon, to Mars, and eventually to the stars.

The alternative is tight quarters and starvation for everyone. Either that or you're going to have to persuade my mother to put up a few houseguests at her house, and I know for a fact she's not going for that.

American Journalism in the 21ˢᵗ Centruy

Editor's note:
Brian Karem became a reporter when he was 20, working for the now defunct Kingdom Daily Sun Gazette in Fulton, Mo. Since leaving the University of Missouri, he has worked as a television reporter, newspaper and magazine reporter, television producer, and has written four books.

In 1990, he became the first journalist in the country to be jailed trying to defend the First Amendment in more than a dozen years. He went to jail four times in a case that has been included in journalism textbooks in the last decade.

He covered the Gulf War, the Branch Davidian standoff, aspects of every presidential race since 1984, and during his career has interviewed virtually everyone on the political spectrum from G. Gordon Liddy to James Carville.

The following essay contains his reflections on his last 20 years as a working reporter. The two essays following it were written at the time they occurred and contain his reflections about news events of which he felt strongly.

M.M.

I AM AFRAID, AND MORE THAN THAT, I am afraid that I don't care any more.

Specifically, I am afraid for my craft, but as I grow older and more concerned for my children and their well-being, I simply can't garner the energy to consider the problems of American Journalism with the vigor I once could. I think I've begun to drown in its absurdities.

I used to go to work with a sense of pride and passion. I was on a mission, and it wasn't a mission to gain fame nor fortune for myself. I really *believed*. Growing up reading Barry Bingham's *Courier Journal* and *Louisville Times* and being exposed to H. L. Mencken at an early age, I came to believe that being a reporter was a calling that required self-sacrifice, brought with it an element of danger, and was ultimately one of the most rewarding professions one could enter. Neither limited to a desk nor shackled to the same experiences day in and day out, a reporter could see and taste and hear an endless variety of experiences during the course of his or her lifetime.

I was naïve thinking this of course, and my naïveté began with my firm belief that a reporter was a "professional" man. For the reporter, no matter the cut of his suit or his style of clothes, no matter whether he works for newspapers, television, radio, or the Internet, is still nothing more than a hired hand. In some cases, like Barbara Walters, an expensive hired hand, but a hired hand nonetheless. Yet, many reporters today believe themselves to be a professional person on the same level as a doctor, lawyer, or more accurately, an actor. We dine at fine restaurants, and the most famous reporters are in the presence of presidents, kings, and the obscenely rich. Yet, one telephone call from his boss can render a reporter helpless, put him out of work, out of sight and out of mind.

"He remains, for all his dreams, a hired man- the owner downstairs, or even the business manager . . . is still free to demand his head- and a hired man is not a professional man. The essence of a professional man is that he is answerable for his professional conduct only to his professional peers," Mencken wrote almost 75 years ago.

Today, this delusion of professionalism has permeated the reporters' ranks to the point that those reporters who toil for high-profile publications like *Time* and *Newsweek*, or high-profile reporters themselves- those anchors and network reporters who live in the limelight- have come to believe they are every bit as important as the story they are covering. They have become celebrities covering other celebrities. In some cases, such as the Washington, D.C., press corps, the distance between the reporters and those we cover have become so small that we've become part of the same insular crowd and therefore compromised ourselves as reporters. In this case, we've not only deluded ourselves into believing we are important professionals, but we've deluded ourselves into believing our opinions matter. Thus, we play tennis with the President or dine regularly with the Secretary of the Treasury, and it becomes just a little more difficult to write or report on our new powerful friends objectively.

Elsewhere, it isn't the news event any more that is important, but the people who tell us about it. It isn't the tragedy at Waco and the Branch Davidians that is as important as is the fact that the fiery visage of David Koresh and his followers were on the cover of every news magazine and being reported with eager enthusiasm by every well-known face on television. Major news events now transcend the merely tragic aspects of life for the viewers and readers, becoming a way to be a voyeur without any of the danger of being called such. For the reporters who cover the events in the field, they also enjoy the added vicarious thrill that one gets in riding a roller coaster. As a reporter, one gets to experience an adrenaline rush as substantial and pulse enhancing as the carnival thrill ride with only a slightly greater chance of actually experiencing something truly horrendous in life- we're front-row voyeurs. More than that, the truly horrendous events of life- the mass murders, the wars, the bombings- become not only vicarious thrill rides for the reporters but also parties at which all reporters get to catch up with their colleagues and discuss the vicissitudes of the latest trendy restaurant or the newest expensive suit. Not only has the medium become the message, but it has become entertainment to package, sell, and advertise. The reporter gets his front row seat and the country club atmosphere of bonding with other reporters who congratulate themselves upon being at the latest trendy cataclysmic event.

It is both curiously invigorating and ultimately disheartening for those adrenaline junkies who joined the ranks of reporters with the vigor and ideals of Barry Bingham Sr. and Robert Worth Bingham, the initial owner of the *Courier Journal* and *Louisville Times*. Above the lobby elevators in the office building that houses the *Courier Journal* and the now defunct *Louisville Times* is a saying attributed to Robert Worth Bingham: "I have always regarded the newspapers owned by me as a public trust and have endeavored so to conduct them as to render the greatest public service."

It is that inspiration, whether the actual quote is known by most reporters, which drove many people to take up the craft. There is, after all, a certain romantic appeal in being a reporter. A reporter does get that wonderful front seat view of history, heinous crimes, the greatest joys and the greatest adventures on Earth. No reporter, save the laziest, need toil away for eight hours in a stuffy office cubicle planning out his life in coffee spoons. He or she can see the world- and usually on someone else's nickel. But, more, and much more than that, as romance has it, the intrepid reporter wears him or herself out trying to get the news to inform the masses. There have been reporters and photographers killed, wounded, or held hostage in every war this country has fought. Many brave men and women have given the ultimate sacrifice in defense of the principle that a well-informed populace is essential and vital to a democracy. "The First Amendment is first for a reason," many reporters have said. Others paraphrase Jefferson and point out that the press is vital to the workings of a democracy, and if stuck with a choice of no newspapers or no government, there are few reporters alive who would choose the latter over the former.

Yet, for all it's pontificating, posturing, and high-handed reasons for existence, the media today are awash in venal, vile, and horribly inept reporters and editors. As in Mencken's time, there are scores of reporters who do not have the bellicosity nor the intelligence to do the job for which they've been hired. Many have no idea what "passive voice" is or how to conjugate a verb. Some are merely faces who smile on television. Some are nephews or children of publishers who never really found themselves. Some are failed lawyers or poets who think they can write. A few are merely horribly incompetent and live each moment in fear that they will be found out to be the frauds they know themselves to be (These are usually editors and news directors). There are scores of reporters who have no idea of the difference between the Bill of Rights and a bill of sale, the Ten Commandments and David Letterman's *Top Ten List*. The very worst of them have not the remotest clue as to why they became reporters nor the vaguest notion of what it means to ask an intelligent question- let alone settle on one intelligent question to ask.

This was dramatically seen and successfully skewered on *Saturday Night Live* during the Gulf War when reporters at the military briefings in Riyadh, Saudi Arabia asked the most inane questions about secret troop movements and battle plans. It has been echoed by Barbara

Walters who was taken to task for her less than stellar performance in interviewing the Ramseys, whose daughter Jon Benet has become the latest media darling in death. It was echoed by Maria Shriver, the angular faced member of the Kennedy clan whose only other claim to fame was in marrying a testosterone-soaked actor. She had the ignorance to ask Senator John McCain the worst question in the world, "How do you feel?" after McCain lost a crucial Republican presidential primary. In a display of arrogance worthy of a Kennedy and a reporter, Shriver and her bosses defended her effort and denounced McCain as being rude despite the fact that McCain asked her to "please" leave him alone.

"It is this vast and militant ignorance, this widespread and fathomless prejudice against intelligence, that makes American Journalism so pathetically feeble and vulgar, and so generally disreputable," Mencken said in 1926.

As the 21st Century comes galloping at us, it will trample us and leave us in its wake to ponder what happened. It has become increasingly apparent that not only have things not gotten any better in the last 75 years of American Journalism, but, indeed, things have gotten quite a bit worse. The root cause of this is not just the ignorant legions of reporters and editors, but the business managers who hire them. They ultimately are responsible for they pull the purse strings and make the policy decisions which dictate how everything runs in the newsroom. The loving attention to the bottom line and the ignorant abandonment of long-term goals and ideals for short-sighted, quick-fix solutions are directly responsible for the increase in infotainment news, false news, staged video, and the proliferation of slogans like "News You Can Use" and "Channel Four on Your Side!"

When the corporations came to understand that news divisions could actually make money for the company, instead of being a loss leader, that was, of course, the beginning of the trek down a very steep and slippery slope. The slide picked up blazing speed as afternoon newspapers began to fail because of the advent of the 6 p.m. newscast and then the slide reached something akin to light speed with the multiplication of media outlets. There are dozens, if not hundreds, of cable and satellite channels. There is the Internet and tabloids, 24-hour news, and NPR. The supply of news has never been greater, but the content, with a few notable exceptions, is far more shallow. The proliferation of all of this media has sparked a rush to market research-driven reporting and the desire to appeal to as many people as possible by whatever means available.

Compounding and aiding in this slide into sleaze is the fact that more and more of the media outlets in this country are owned by fewer and fewer people. These large behemoths have no need nor desire for anything more than the most facile reporting. These Corporate Suits just want a product that sells. So, there is a real and very democracy-threatening possibility that truly independent voices will be drowned out, driven out, and quashed by multi-national corporations whose greatest concern is the amount of return on investment for each stockholder. I do not condemn the pursuit of happiness via the accumulation of wads of sweaty cash, but I still naively believe there are some things which have nothing to do with the bottom line. Reporting the news should be one of those.

There are other by-products equally harmful to journalism that are inherent in large corporate ownership. Political correctness has taken over as corporations rush to make sure there is no sexual harassment, racial or other discrimination. But far from dealing with those problems in any manner that resembles common sense, corporations have decided to deal with these very real problems by steps so drastic and ludicrous as to seem Draconian or invented by the mind of one of the Three Stooges. In this, newsrooms are not alone. Things have swung so far in our striving not to anger or offend anyone that in news and other offices across the country, off-color jokes can be interpreted as sexual or racial discrimination. As in other large corporate environments, the mere hint of anything resembling racial or sexual harassment- whether it be in the form of a horrible joke, an off-color comment or the scratching of certain areas of the body in public- can lead to the end of a career. In an industry which exists because of the First Amendment, ironically it has become increasingly impossible to exercise the First Amendment. In this country, the prevailing attitude used to be, "I may disagree with what you say, but I will defend to death your right to say it." Today, especially in corporate journalism, the prevailing attitude is, "I may disagree in public (in private, I probably agree with you) with what you say and will cause your death (professional or otherwise) if you say it."

Further, in television, racial profiling has gone to extremes as each station attempts to have on-air reporters and anchors who fit into neat little ethnic categories. There is the token white guy, the token black guy and the token woman- who if African American also fills another niche. In some parts of the country, there is the token Hispanic, Asian, and the ubiquitous ex-jock in sports. Sometimes a token hairdo, either male or female, will also inhabit the weather anchor spot, although that seems to be the last hiding place for real talent. Most weather people have to know what saturation vapor pressure is, and, because most weather anchors actually know what it is they are talking about, it is no coincidence that the weather segment is the most watched on the local news- even if your local weathercaster can never accurately predict how much snow will fall.

The result of this is a stifling of all creative, independent, and unique thought. To think becomes akin to offending, and to offend in the modern office environment is anathema. Thus, in reporting, the corporate mentality has led to pack journalism and news release journalism. Far from wearing oneself out to get the news as romance has it, reporters today have slipped supinely into the estate and dignity of a comatose couch potato. It's easy, it's fast and takes no effort and little thought, but it certainly pleases the bosses who have no desire to anger the Suits in the corporate offices. It's become very easy, therefore, to fill a one-minute gap in the local news or 12 inches of copy in the local newspaper by making a few calls and re-writing a news release. False news, incorrectly spelled names, and wholesale fabrications thus proliferate under the banner of efficiency.

Witness, for the example, the group called I.R.E. - Investigative Reporters and Editors. It has been around for many years now and was formed by a group of investigative reporters in the wake of the Watergate Scandal. In the early 1980s, a national convention of IRE resembled a meeting of the Ross Perot fan club. The numbers were exceedingly small, but the group was dedicated to the preservation of hardcore investigative reporting. Topics of discussion at one of its first national conventions included how to file freedom of information requests, how to search for proper documentation of government malfeasance, how to find out if benzene and other heavy metals were present in your drinking water. By the end of the last century, the numbers had swollen at national IRE conventions to the thousands, but the topics of discussion had then come to include the best use of hidden camera video (a

41

discussion not-so-curiously limited to "gee, if it looks good then use it"). Other stories discussed were about how to test to see if automatic car washes were dispensing the right amount of soap, and how to make sure you were getting the right amount of cheese on your take-out pizza. There were still discussions about hardcore investigative reporting, but they had been overcome by the banal and tedious stories populating television news.

It had become too expensive and too time-consuming to engage in real investigative reporting. Real investigative reporting takes time, cannot be quantified, and runs the risk of angering not only investors, but other viewers. In addition, angry viewers definitely have a greater chance of bringing on lawsuits. Those lawsuits can come from other corporations whose pockets are just as deep if not more so than the corporation that owns the television station or newspaper that originally aired or printed the investigative report. Bean counters long ago decided that only the lawyers make any money in that scenario, so, hey, why go to the trouble of investigating anything and take money out of the hands of the stockholders?

Consequently, investigative reports on television have diminished in their scope while at the same time increasing in their numbers. Reporters have been requested to air one to as many as five stories a week under the banner of "investigative reporting." The corporate mentality has thus grasped the concept that an investigative report can garner additional viewers and consequently bring in more advertising revenue, but the Corporate Suits have decided that investigative reporting must conform to market realities. The bottom line, of course, is that a story about too little soap in the automatic car wash is much easier to produce than a story about the possibility that bovine growth hormone which is present in a lot of milk you buy at the supermarket may cause cancer.

In addition, the quick and easy story must necessarily be both lurid and shallow or at least have the appearance of being lurid. The Corporate Suits are then appeased on at least three levels. There is marketable and hopefully profitable investigative reporting being done. It appeals to the market research which shows that audiences like to hear that investigative reporting is being done, and finally it appeals to the corporate lawyers who would much rather deal with a local car wash than another multi-national company embroiled in scandalous and ultimately potentially expensive litigious activities.

This bastardization of news has spread like a cancer through television and has made its way into newspapers as well, many of which have decided that real investigative reporting was simply too much for the reader to read and too time-consuming to undertake. There are of course exceptions to this, but they do remain few if notable.

Also, as time has progressed, in many cases, the tools a reporter needs to become a good investigative reporter have not been taught let alone honed- especially in television. A physically-attractive reporter may be something to look at on camera, but a college degree in physical education is scarcely adequate to do the job. It also used to take years of work for a reporter to gain the title or the responsibility of investigative reporting. One needed to work a beat and get to know sources before one attempted to do something as difficult as an investigative piece. City editors were notorious for handing out investigative assignments like juicy, plump plums. Now, since the level of reporting has been lowered, those who are pressed into service are not of the same quality as those they've replaced. But it scarcely matters to the bean counters as long as the station or the newspaper continues to turn a profit.

The horror is that many of the lawsuits the Corporate Suits fear would be erased if competent people were left to their own devices. I've never heard of a business manager in either television or newspaper who got upset when the flood of complaints about inaccuracies, bad spelling, and out right falsehoods ceased to come into his or her office on a daily basis.

The shame of it is that many of the evils of Journalism could be addressed if only imaginative and competent individuals were running the news departments. But imaginative and competent individuals scare the newspaper business managers and the television station managers. Such a man or woman is hard to control. Men and women who fear for their jobs and grovel upon demand as corporations dangle financial security over their heads are much better suited for news management because these reporters and editors are far easier to manipulate and ultimately much more expendable. A news manager out of work may have a difficult time getting back into the game, but there are dozens if not hundreds of similar-minded drones standing in line behind the ousted news executive ready to take his or her place.

Stupidity runs rampant through the hallowed halls of Journalism these days, but there are few frank and open discussions of the evils threatening Journalism in this country. We are far too willing to pat ourselves on the back, or in the case of certain aging network anchors, too willing to Big Foot a story and stand in the foxhole of a soldier and declare that they are reporting from "the forward most position in the American lines" during the Gulf War.

American Journalism has become inundated with reporters and editors who are so enamored of their own self-worth that critical observation about their craft has become difficult if not impossible. These are small-minded men and women who aspire to nothing greater than to be the king of their own private dung hill. "The rewards of their trade used to come in freedom, opportunity, the incomparable delights of self-expression: now they come in money," Mencken wrote. In television, though, there is a far more insidious evil that permeates everything that is done by reporters and anchors- it is the joy of seeing oneself on the small screen. A beginning reporter in some of the nation's smaller and even medium television markets does not make as much as their counterparts in advertising sales, nor do they make as much as the technicians who keep the television station on the air. Some of these reporters and anchors do not even make as much as managers of fast food chains, yet they get something none of the aforementioned people get: they get to see themselves on television, and, in doing so, they become something of a minor local celebrity themselves. It may mean a wink or a nod of recognition at public events, at church, or in the grocery store. It may mean someone asking them for their autograph, or it may mean the occasional free ticket to a concert or other public event. It is this lure, greater than money, which draws the mediocre and truly banal into television and makes it such a desert of quality. "Look at me! Look at me!" television reporters say with aplomb. Nobody but their families seem to care.

The poor newspaper and radio reporters don't even get that. They often get a smaller salary and less notoriety. Is it any wonder that American Journalism is therefore populated by morons, boobs and miscreants of all sorts? And once locked into a career in journalism, what reporter today will rock the boat? Like a smack junkie, the reporter becomes addicted to the adrenaline rush of major news events, the ability to go anywhere and be anywhere whenever needed. The rush of deadline is like a syringe full of heroin and the lure is just as tragic. Once inside the great beast, to rock the boat is to face the possibility of imminent unemployment. For a young reporter making nothing and just starting out, who wants to rock the boat and miss the ride? For those who've been in the business for a while, who wants to rock the boat and lose the retirement benefits, life and health insurance and risk being branded as a loose cannon? What reporter, editor, or anchor making top dollar wants to rock the boat and miss out on the notoriety, great salary, and the joy of being recognized in public? Few want to face that challenge and fewer still even realize that it is a challenge to face.

That's why more and more the only place to find the best investigative reporting any more is the *National Enquirer*.

Now you understand why I'm really afraid.

*Of Politicians
and The Press*
*(Or: Why Can't
Johnny Think?)*

Politicians and hypocrisy are as common as journalists and hypocrisy. They are also just about as much fun to write about.

I DETEST WHINERS. Under this category I have recently added the group of concerned journalists who are whining about Republican Susan Molinari jumping the congressional ship for the floundering CBS frigate, and Robert Reich, President Clinton's first-term labor secretary.

Reich makes this list for his sophomoric reply to the *Washington Post* over the controversy that the *National Journal's* Jonathan Rauch began when he critiqued Reich's autobiography, *Locked in the Cabinet*, portions of which were excerpted in the *Post*. At issue with Reich is the contention that he apparently made up quotes, scenes, and dialogue in his autobiography to enhance the dramatic conflict of his narrative. Reich offers no coherent defense of this abhorrent practice. Rather he sheepishly says he is no investigative reporter and is merely offering up his memoirs to the public.

" . . . these are my perceptions," he told Rauch. "This is the way I experienced it."

Apparently, the way Reich felt things happened and the way they, in fact, did happen are miles apart. When called on the carpet for this questionable practice, Reich merely decided in good political and bureaucratic from to shoot the journalistic messenger. Reich refers to Rauch as his "executioner" in his reply to the *Post* and says, even though he was a respected and supposedly responsible member of government, he felt no responsibility to check the "official public record" to see if his memoir was factually accurate. In the past, when someone's recollection of events veered as dangerously far from reality as Reich's apparently did, a good bit of psychoanalysis would seem to be in order. Now, we just put these people in government and give them big advance checks for their memoirs.

I'm sorry, Mr. Reich, but this is not the type of social responsibility I wish to impart to my children. Reich's simplistic "And that's the truth" statement at the end of his letter to the *Post* resonated with the juvenile aplomb of a Lily Tomlin/Edith Ann tirade. I strongly suspect sticking his tongue out and going "Thfffpt" is more than implied. Even though you claim you are no journalist, you were acting as one when you wrote your memoirs, and you do have a responsibility to seek out and print the facts. All your whining does not hide the fact that you failed to do so.

With that said, I'm horrified that we have another politician wading into the muddied journalistic waters. But, then, we have no one but ourselves to blame for Susan Molinari coming to CBS News; and while we should not expect any more out of her than we got from Mr. Reich, we should quit whining about this problem and do something about it.

The issue is quite simple, and it has nothing to do with partisan politics as Mrs. Molinari's supporters claim. Andrew Heyward, president of CBS News, lives in the real world where ratings and money matter. Today, the quickest way to get both is to hire someone with his or her own celebrity attached to his or her name. It also doesn't hurt that Mrs. Molinari is a Republican and CBS can use her to deflect the "Liberal Media" cry of the magpies known as *g. gordon liddy americanus*.

"We're gutless. We're spineless," CBS anchor Dan Rather told the *Boston Herald* in September 1991. "There's no joy in saying this, but beginning in the 1980s, the American press by and large somehow began to operate on the theory that the first order of business was to be popular with the person, or organization or institution that you cover."

I wonder how Mr. Rather feels about cozying up to Mrs. Molinari?

"There is in all history, " H. L. Mencken wrote more than 70 years ago, "no record of a newspaper owner who complained because his paper was well-edited. And I know of no business manager who objected when the complaints pouring in upon him, of misrepresentations, invasions of privacy, gross inaccuracies and other such nuisances, began to lighten."

The public knows we're not doing our job. It takes no genius to see this. The rest of America are tuning us out. The numbers of people watching the network nightly news continue to drop, newspaper circulation declines, the actual number of newspapers in operation grows smaller and all we do is complain that Susan Molinari shouldn't be an anchor for CBS.

Of course she shouldn't. We have brought ourselves to this low point in journalism by failing to do our jobs. We cannot just blame our editors, our news directors, the money men nor our network executives. We can only blame the proximate man. For if we did our jobs right- without partisan rancor- and we worked hard to make this perception known to the public, instead of cozying up to those in power as Mr. Rather pointed out, then perhaps Andrew Heyward could afford to hire a real journalist.

Looked at in this light, Mrs. Molinari's hiring makes perfect business sense and it is useless to wring our hands or gnash our teeth about it. In fact, with Mrs. Molinari now working for CBS, it isn't too far fetched to think we may soon see Mr. Reich with his own network news show- *News as I See It.* Perhaps there's room on the "eye" network for that bit of fiction and fantasy- paired with Mrs. Molinari's Saturday morning show, my children may not decry the loss of their Saturday morning cartoons after all.

Speaking of the Truth

Hypocrisy and the media are married, joined at the hip, improbable but constantly strange bedfellows. Pick your cliché and it works. The hypocrisy in my chosen profession is also one of my favorite subjects to write about, only because it is so deliciously fun.

A QUICK RECAP FOR THOSE OF us who may have forgotten: CNN airs a story maintaining that during the Vietnam War the U.S. military used deadly sarin gas on American defectors. It turns out the story, if not entirely fabricated, was at the very least questionable enough that it shouldn't have aired as it was.

The reporter, the man everyone actually saw on the television set delivering the exercise in journalistic fantasy, was none other than Peter Arnett. He of Gulf War fame. He of stoic mannerism, serious journalism, and unquestionable wisdom told us perhaps one of the biggest journalistic tall tales since H. L. Mencken purposely perpetrated the "Great Bathtub Hoax"- or at least since Mr. Phil Glass (which reminds me of Seymour Glass and J. D. Salinger but that's another story) perpetrated numerous hoaxes at the *New Republic*. Phil was fired. Peter was not.

Arnett's defense? He had, in the immortal words of Richard Pryor, "Nuthin' to do with it. I wasn't even in the vicinity." Arnett claimed he just parachuted in (his words), asked the questions he was told to ask, voiced the piece, and then, I guess, worried about where he might have lunch. On the basis of this, CNN reprimanded him, but let him keep his job.

According to Huey Strong, the managing editor at the highly

respected *Houston Post*, this is tantamount to "saying as a doctor I had nothing to do with the brain surgery so don't sue me for malpractice." Sure. He further explained, "I was the surgeon of record, but I did little more than show up and smile. Don't sue me because the patient died."

Tommy Borders, the executive editor of the prestigious *Louisville Times*, says it is another case of television reporters being little more than talking head actors, selling credibility with a wrinkled brow, serious gesture and staid mannerisms. "We could never get away with such trivial flippancy in print," Borders says. "The defense Mr. Arnett offers is grounds for termination in my book. This is just another example of how television is blurring the lines of journalism and gossip. We're no longer viewed by our public as purveyors of truth. Rather, we've become the purveyors of sleaze, tripe, and allegory. Mr. Arnett has done a terrible disservice to our profession, and I for one will never watch CNN again." Short of urging a boycott of CNN, Borders says he will never consider hiring anyone who has worked for the organization.

But those in television who've had to withstand the disdain of their print brothers for years point to the *New Republic* debacle and say those in glass houses shouldn't throw stones. "Hey, in this drive to compete and get the juiciest stuff on the air or in print, newspapers and magazines are at fault, too," says Ted Chaoby, the executive producer at WHTP in Denver. "Long ago, we abandoned the moral high ground and people know it. Only the dinosaurs in print refuse to believe it. They'll soon go the way of the Dodo bird anyway, so who cares?"

Meanwhile, those at the Center for Advanced Sociology Studies think that all journalists are just being short-sighted. "Jack Reed, the man upon whose life the movie *Reds* is based, he himself admitted to occasionally fudging facts for the greater good of clarity and truth," says Seymour Kearney, the director of the Center. "We have become so literal, so determined to use facts that we forget the devil is in the details. Facts can obscure the truth rather than bring light to it." Kearney points to the *Cincinnati Inquirer* story that highlighted problems with the giant Chiquita Banana empire. The reporter in question may have stolen some of the information he used in a story, but "that doesn't mean the information was wrong or bad. It just means the reporter didn't conform to fact gathering mores to put together his story. This is as strong an example of short-sighted fuzzy thinking as exists in the world of journalism today with the possible exception of Peter Arnett." Kearney also notes the viewing public is getting sold a bill of goods by television producers who use reporters as "front men." Gone, he says, "are the glory days when reporters actually did their own work and stood behind what they put on the air. It's a sad comment on the integrity of the business as a whole."

There is little doubt that traditional media sources must stem the tide with more scrupulous and thorough reporting. Some would like to attack the fringe players in the journalism world by trying to define what a real reporter is. Some have even thought of licensing reporters like automobile drivers- a chilling thought for those of us who simply want our First Amendment rights. So, where does the viewer and the reader fall in all of this? With things like the Drudge Report and *Ain't It Cool News* on the Internet, viewers and readers are finding themselves inundated daily with rumor, innuendo and opinions parading as facts through which they must wade with an increasingly jaundiced eye.

Perhaps once again we should listen to H. L. Mencken's words as he spoke of journalists: "He prints balderdash because he doesn't know how to get anything better- perhaps, in many cases, because he doesn't know that anything better exists . . . It is not that he is dishonest, but that he is stupid- and, being stupid, a coward." Ponder that for a while. This came from the man who made up an entire history of bathtubs, published it, had it reprinted as gospel around the country and then had to spend years telling everyone it was just a joke- and weren't they smart enough to see that? Well, no. Not then and not now. Perhaps never.

And in the spirit of H.L. Mencken let me just add that except for the underlying facts and Mencken's quote, which come from his *Prejudices: Sixth Series* (Alfred A. Knopf, Inc., 1927), I made the rest of this up.

Now, go home and think.

The Politics of Truth

This article first appeared in San Antonio magazine, September, 1989.

The Politics of Truth
Can It Keep the Media Honest?

A free press can of course be good or bad, but, most certainly, without freedom it will never be anything but bad.
-Albert Camus

IT ALL STARTED because of my professional curiosity. My mother used to call it nosiness, but since I now make a living at such things I can call it my "professional curiosity."

Anyway, what is at issue is an interview I got with a man accused of killing a San Antonio police officer. It was not just any police officer, mind you, but Gary Lee Williams. The very same Gary Lee Williams who it later was determined had traces of cocaine and heroin in his blood stream at the time of his death.

All of this got started on March 27, 1989, at about 3 a.m. It is alleged, and has been reported, that it was at this time that 25-year-old Henry David Hernandez, along with his 27-year-old brother Julian, shot officer Williams with his own gun on a routine traffic stop. More specifically, police say the pair scuffled with Williams for an unspecified reason, took his gun away from him and shot him twice and then fled.

I, along with every other police reporter in town, wrote that story and then sat and waited as the police department, naturally riled

61

because one of their officers had been slain with his own gun, went about the task of trying to find the pair responsible.

We didn't have to wait long. In the afternoon of March 28, we received a telephone call at KMOL-TV from the district attorney's office. We were being invited to his office to witness Henry David and Julian Hernandez turn themselves in to district attorney Fred Rodriguez.

The district attorney has a sense of fair play about these things, so obviously every other media outlet in town was also invited to this ceremony. However, despite the nice invitation, most of the members of the media were treated rather rudely by the D.A.'s staff once we got there. We were all pushed around by about a dozen men guarding the Hernandez brothers as they were rushed to Judge James Barlow's court for arraignment. Inside the courtroom, Joe Hernandez, their attorney but of no relation, told Judge Barlow, " . . . They request they not be interviewed by any member of the police department without counsel being present. We ask the court to enforce that particularly."

I was understandably curious about that, or yes, even nosy. Apparently, what it meant was although the two had turned themselves in, no one- except maybe their attorney- had found out their side of the story.

Those thoughts had little time to grow as the pair were quickly ushered out of the courtroom and back down the hall where the D.A.'s storm troopers began throwing body blocks against the members of the media. Apparently, someone hadn't told them we were invited. In the ensuing scramble, one female reporter nearly had her arm removed from her shoulder socket. I got a nasty gash in my almost-expensive black pinstripe suit and a photographer for KENS-TV was introduced to the door of the D.A.'s office in a most abrupt manner.

After the fracas, the reporters and photographers left. But it seemed that a lot of questions remained unanswered. Who actually did the shooting, one or both brothers? Did they participate together in the assault on the police officer? How and why did the fight start? Investigators had not found officer William's gun. Where was it? Was it self-defense? I mean, I never knew Gary Williams, but I have known some police officers who like to bust heads.

Those were compelling enough questions, considering that officer Williams became the third police officer shot in as many weeks, for me to try and find the answers. It was a story, I believe, of overwhelming interest to the community at the time it happened. But, if we all waited until the case went to court months down the line, who would remember or care, other than the immediate family and friends of those directly involved? Besides, I've often found that information received in the sanitized environment of a courtroom is not always accurate or without the spins and twists attorneys put on it for purposes of prosecuting or defending someone. Finally, I just had to know for myself because it seemed the entire police department, or at least a good number of people in homicide, were upset with the district attorney because the brothers turned themselves in to him, instead of them. My nosiness/ curiosity got the better of me. What was going on?

When I got back to the station that afternoon, I found out I wasn't the only one interested in getting Herandez' side of the story on the air. According to some of his relatives, Henry David wanted to talk to the media. Anyway, at 7:20 p.m. or so on March 28th, Henry David Hernandez called me at KMOL. For about 15 minutes, I talked to him before he told me he had to go. Later, he called me back and we talked some more. During our two conversations, he told me that he had pulled the trigger that had killed Williams. His brother, I was told, was never involved in the shooting and the officer was only shot once, not twice as had been claimed by the police department. Hernandez claimed that a neck wound the police reported to be a superficial gunshot wound was actually a bite wound. A fact that the medical examiner would later corroborate.

According to the outtakes of our taped conversation, which now rest with the state- although I was not in favor of turning them over- this is how Henry David Hernandez remembered the confrontation.

Brian: *The first shot hit him in the neck?*
Henry: *Uh, that shot? That didn't hit him in the neck. The bullet went to the other direction . . . he didn't get shot twice. Because the first bullet went towards the back of me. Because I took away the gun, up. And it was back and it was boom and then he charged at me. Then I dropped him down one time.*

As I said, Henry David's side of the story ran that night along with what the police department said happened. Not too many days afterwards came the subpoenas and the court appearances, the bickering and the backbiting.

I'm going to summarize the events that followed as succinctly as possible. I was questioned by police the next day and in my statement I carefully kept out any references to who helped me arrange that interview with Hernandez. After all, the man was in jail when he called me and someone had to let him know that I was as interested in listening to his side of the story as he was in telling it. According to one homicide detective, that bit of information would be the thing the prosecutor would most want to know.

During my first court appearance that quickly became a topic for debate.

"I need to know if this man, Brian Karem, was acting as an agent of the State. It makes a lot of difference in my investigation and my indicting of these folks. I need to know the information," Assistant District Attorney Beth Taylor said in court.

Needless to say, I think that is rubbish. As far as I know, only KMOL-TV pays my salary. I also know, from being at the crime scene, that there were witnesses to the shooting and material evidence that linked the two brothers to the slaying. I found it hard to believe that Taylor needed my source to indict the Hernandez brothers. (It also turned out later that she got an indictment without my source.) I asked her about that in court:

Brian- *It is my understanding, from the information I received from the police department, which you should well have, and I am sure you already do, there were ... witnesses at the scene. Why would this information be needed by you?*

Ms. Taylor: *You don't tell me how to run my case.*

Brian: *Well, I'm asking.*

Ms. Taylor: *You don't ask what my information is. That is not your job.*

Of course, that is my job. In fact, asking people like Beth Taylor questions is what makes my job fun. Anyway, I get ahead of myself. We were subpoenaed for tapes and notes- including our outtakes which everyone in television journalism considers the equivalent of notes. We handed over the outtakes against my will. But, when it came down to notes the station management agreed with me- we could not turn them over because confidential sources were being protected. The management backed up their resolve with legal assistance. I had to protect those sources. I've said many times (and I do firmly believe) that all you have in this business is your credibility. If you break promises, if you're not a man of your word, then you have no more credibility than the chronic liar (You also won't get many exclusive stories, and in my case, my professional curiosity would rarely be satisfied).

But all of that aside, the deeper issue is the First Amendment. Today, I find it in peril. A free press cannot really be free if you cannot obtain information. Many people are justifiably worried about going on the record in some instances. Although I don't like to use anonymous sources, they are sometimes necessary to the free flow of information. If those sources dry up because people are afraid I'll have to turn over their names in court, then freedom of the press means little- about as much as it means in Soviet Russia.

That idea should not be foreign to Mark Stevens or Gerald Goldstein. They are the defense lawyers for Henry David Hernandez and Julian Hernandez, respectively. More importantly, as far as I'm concerned, they also do a lot of work for the American Civil Liberties Union.

It was damn strange, to say the least, to find men who've so vociferously fought for the First Amendment, trying to put it aside in my case. In fact, Goldstein sounded so much like a prosecutor in the first hearing that at one point Judge Barlow even stopped to ask him if he was sure of what side he was on.

Stevens, though, was not without his bright spots. One of his assertions all along has been that the information I have could not be obtained from any other source- as if his client had suddenly become mute and couldn't tell him what he told me, or who passed him the note in jail with my name and telephone number on it. I tried to bring that up during court, much to Stevens' chagrin I'm sure:

Brian: *Excuse me. May I ask a question at this point?*
Barlow: *Uh-huh.*
Brian: *You say we can't get it from any other source. The information I got was from your client. You have no greater access to your client than I do?*
Mr. Goldstein: *It is not my client.*
Mr. Stevens: *It is my client.*
Brian: *You have no greater access to your client than I do?*
Mr. Stevens: *You don't get to ask questions.*

I guess the fact I asked the judge permission to ask Stevens a question meant nothing to him since I was found in contempt of court for refusing to turn over my notes. I submit Stevens should also be found in contempt of court for failing to answer my question.

The first hearing concluded on May 10th with me refusing to turn over my notes. The judge, as I already said, found me in civil contempt of court and sentenced me to six months in jail. He fined me too (adding insult to injury since we all know reporters are paid about as well as teachers). That night on television you probably saw me with handcuffs on, wearing my black pinstripe suit I believe (It had recently been repaired after the fiasco the day the Hernandez brothers were arraigned).

I got to go to jail, have my fingerprints taken along with my mug shot, and I got to sit and go through a lot of questions while the hookers in one of the jail cells beckoned for me. Luckily, I was taken up on the seventh floor in the security area where they keep the Mexican Mafia and Texas Syndicate. It's safer there. I stayed about two and a half hours in jail the first time, and on the following Friday, I stayed about five hours after Judge Barlow had a rehearing and I again respectfully declined to turn over my notes. The newspapers have had some fun with this. One front page columnist even managed two columns out of it, although he never once called and talked to me about it. I found that a "difficult, if fascinating, situation," to use his words.

"On the one hand, we don't like alleged cop killers," he said of print journalists. "On the other, we like TV reporters even less."

It certainly is nice to see that in the grand scheme of things, I fit in somewhere just under alleged cop killers. Oh well, at least I know where I stand.

That same newspaper also ran an analysis piece that devoted about eight column inches to my story. The reporter who wrote that dribble also never called to talk to me about it, and like the columnist, he never covered the story either. But I find it comforting he thought so much about it he had to analyze it.

At one point, the reporter who was the author of this fanciful and fabricated piece questioned whether I acted responsibly in airing the interview with Hernandez. I've already outlined the ethical and legitimate journalistic reasons why I went after the interview, so that need not be discussed again. The question I want answered from this reporter is if Henry David Hernandez had called him, would he have not done the story? Would his paper have refused to run the story?

Given the *National Enquirer* mentality that prevails at both local newspapers, the newspaper reporter's question is not only stupid, but hypocritical as well.

A lot of water has flowed under the bridge since I got that interview. I found that Judge Barlow thought the fight over my notes was as ludicrous as I believed it to be. I still don't like that he threw me in jail, but I found common ground with him just the same.

I also found common ground with Stevens and Goldstein and was relieved that they at least had ambivalent feelings about going after me. The one person I haven't talked to who had a principal role in this little theatre of the absurd production is Beth Taylor. I guess I should, but I hear she's a cat lover so I don't know if it's possible to find common ground with her.

The biggest revelation, of course, since that interview has been that Williams have been "speedballing," (taking cocaine and heroin) at the time of death-the same ugly drug combination that killed John Belushi. Hernandez's claims that Williams had "an attitude problem" and acted as if he wanted to "hit somebody and keep hitting them" certainly has to be seen in a new light. It also makes the interview with Hernandez more compelling and all that more important. It drives home something basic many of us, including myself, sometimes forget: whenever possible, a reporter must try to get both sides of the story.

Finally, since I first got that interview, I've grown even more sensitive to infringements on First Amendment rights, and I've sat and watched as politicians have wrapped themselves in the flag and denounced those who would otherwise desecrate it. I've also watched as politicians have threatened to slash funds to the National Endowment for the Arts because they don't like someone else's idea of art.

I'm not defending flag burners, or those artists who would urinate in a jar and call it art, but while I may disagree with what they have to say, I will defend to death their right to say it. That idea founded this country. It is why the First Amendment is first. If we continue to undermine it, we weaken the foundation on which this country was built. It is not my intention to sit around and watch the whole house of cards tumble.

*One Local Reporter's
Tale of War*

This article first appeared in Electronic Media, *April 22, 1991.*

One local reporter's tale of war

Editor's note: *Brian Karem, a reporter for NBC affiliate KMOL-TV in San Antonio, spent three weeks in Saudi Arabia, Iraq and Kuwait covering the war in the Mideast. In this first-person account, he offers a local reporter's perspective on dealing with the military, the desert and the war.*

The major newspapers and TV networks leveled plenty of criticism at the military's handling of reporters during the Persian Gulf War. But at least they could get someone to listen to them.

I can still see Col. Larry Icenogle, a pit bull in uniform, ready to lash out at me at the Joint Information Bureau at the Dhahran International Hotel.

"What are you doing here?" he snapped.

"I mean, why are you here? The networks are here. The big dogs are all here. I don't have time for you. You're a little dog."

I had the audacity to think I was in Saudi Arabia to talk to Texans involved in Operation Desert Storm, since my employer, KMOL-TV, had spent what my news director considers a small fortune getting me and another reporter to Dhahran.

The trip cost KMOL more than $15,000 for airfare, hotel, a car, phone bills and living expenses for three weeks.

Fellow reporter Gabe Caggiano and I had traveled to Jeddah, Saudi Arabia, via British Airways. But in Jeddah, I had to fight with Saudi

Airline officials to get us on a plane to Riyadh.

Our reservations were no good because when the war broke out Saudi Airlines cut back its Jeddah-to-Riyadh flights from 20 a day to three.

The immense weight of the camera equipment didn't make them any happier either. They were proposing a weight penalty that cost more than I'd paid to fly from Houston to London.

I managed to bargain that down to $50 since every price is arguable in Saudi Arabia except the price of gasoline.

However, despite my haggling, I couldn't get Gabe and me on the same plane. We took two different flights that were scheduled to land in Riyadh minutes apart.

I flew in comfort aboard a nice Boeing 747, just me, the other passengers and a small four-legged creature several rows behind me. I never got a good look at it, but because of the sounds it made, I'm sure it was a goat.

We landed in Riyadh and after two skycaps fought with each other over who would carry our luggage and spilled our camera gear and clothes onto the floor of the airport terminal, Gabe and I drove to Dhahran.

For the next four days I did battle with Col. Icenogle and the JIB.

My goal was to visit the 41st Combat Support Hospital from Fort Sam Houston. I had mail for the unit's commander and executive officer. I had an invitation to visit the unit as well.

Since I had visited with the unit in November when its members deployed to Saudi Arabia, and since I consider the unit commander a personal friend, I didn't think I'd have any problem getting an escort to see him.

We all knew I wasn't going to get to see the unit by myself.

The JIB was fond of telling me how many checkpoints there were and the International Hotel's community of journalists had plenty of horror stories of reporters being held at gunpoint by angry MPs who apparently were as eager to shoot reporters as any Iraqi.

So I'd placed my faith in Col. Icenogle and a host of others at the JIB. Now he was giving me a lecture on why I should have stayed home.

This came about because I'd just finished my own lecture to the colonel on the lack of honesty at the JIB.

While Col. Icenogle had been scrupulously honest with me, others at the JIB had not. Earlier in the day someone had told me that he'd finally been able to contact the 41st, and they didn't want to see me.

Since the unit commander's wife had talked with her husband within the last week and told him I was coming with a care package for him that included a half dozen cans of his favorite smoked oysters, I didn't buy the JIB's claim.

"We can't find them," another colonel told me.

"What do you mean you can't find them?" I asked.

"We have no communication with them. They're just out there somewhere."

The next day was the last day I played by the JIB"s rules.

I was told to be at the Dhahran International Airport with gear at 10 a.m. to visit the 114th Evac Hospital with a reluctant JIB escort.

That trip never materialized. My partner and I got to the airport only to be yanked from the tarmac by an MP.

It seems the JIB had decided against the trip. The hospital had casualties and didn't want us to visit.

With my MP escort in tow, I went back to the JIB. Since this was more than a week before the ground war was to begin, I questioned what casualties this hospital could have that would be so overwhelming that they couldn't let us visit for a few hours.

A nice major told me not to ask those kinds of questions.

"That's one of those things we can't answer," he said.

Furious, I gathered my helmet, flak jacket and poncho given to me by the JIB.

I went downstairs to the NBC bureau and got the four-wheel drive vehicle they'd been kind enough to rent for us.

I hopped in and drove with my MP escort back to the Dhahran airport to pick up my partner and our equipment.

"This can't be good news," Gabe said when he saw me.

"Hop in, we're driving north."

I turned and looked at the MP.

"Want to come along?"

All he did was laugh.

Now, to get to where the story was, we had to drive the equivalent of a trip from Houston to Dallas, via San Antonio. That's about 700 miles.

For the next two weeks I ran more than 100 checkpoints on Tapline Road. The first time, after consulting with French reporters, who I was told were experts in the art of checkpoint running, I took 12 hours to drive to Rafha from Dhahran.

I was never even challenged by a guard at any checkpoint.

The 41st was located not for from Rafha.

Though the Army didn't know that, according to JIB, the unit commander had told his wife in a telephone call just days before that I could find him near there.

After my first visit with the 41st, I returned to the JIB in Dhahran and gave them a letter granting me permission to visit the unit, written on the 41st computer and signed by the commander.

"How did you get this?" asked the officer there.

"What do you care? Just process it."

"Well, it'll take at least three to four weeks. We don't do unilaterals here."

We managed to see the 41st two more times before the ground war broke out.

Our services came in handy for NBC, which used our video more than once.

Bur after a while this routine got to us. We became more and more tired as we raced up and down the dangerous blacktop looking for Texans.

I awoke around 4 o'clock one morning, still driving. My car had swerved off the highway into the sand.

I jerked the steering wheel hard to the right and jumped back onto the highway. Gabe, who was asleep on the passenger's side woke up and asked what had happened.

"Jackals," I said.

He just rolled over and went back to sleep. It wasn't until the next day that either one of us questioned my statement.

We traveled with the 41st for the first three days of the ground war, spending most of our time behind two trucks in a nine-mile-long convoy.

I counted my blessings and prayed the Iraqis really didn't have any airpower in reserve. The convoy would have been a tempting sight for a pilot.

It was here that I decided never again to criticize the Army-issue MRE's, or "Meals Ready to Eat," which some soldiers referred to as "Meals Refused by Ethiopians."

Not only were they the only food available, but even with the bottled water we had with us, the things sat rather nicely in your stomach. You found yourself able to hold bowel movements for three days with no problem.

This came in handy since there were no bathrooms anywhere.

We got a ride back to our rental car from some friendly National Guard helicopter pilots who probably felt sorry for our blistered, battered, sandy souls.

I had wondered how I'd keep myself clean in the desert. Sand blasting, it turns out, does an adequate job.

When we got back to the Algosaibi Hotel in Dhahran, we showered, shaved and then loaded three 20-gallon drums with gasoline and put those in our car with some MRE's and two cases of bottles water.

On Feb. 28 we traveled into Kuwait. I crossed the border at the very same point where CBS's Bob Simon and his crew had been picked up several weeks earlier.

It was about 2 a.m. when I crossed. An MP in a hum-vee (military lingo for one of those new wide-bodied jeeps) stopped me. I asked him for directions to Kuwait City.

He told me I was on the right road and to be careful because there were land mines all over the place.

There were numerous bomb craters in the highway and a trip that normally took two or three hours stretched into six.

We saw artillery fire several times along the highway and the ubiquitous oil fires burned like something from the apocalypse for hundreds of miles.

But not once did I get stopped and asked to turn back by a U.S. soldier.

This came after I'd been warned by the JIB that under no circumstances would the media be allowed into Kuwait without a military escort.

This had been a joke to many of us, since some network crews had made it into Kuwait City ahead of the military.

I found that the soldiers in the field were more understanding than

I'd been led to believe.

They just wanted their mail and news from home. I just wanted to let the folks know how they were doing.

I got that done and am happy to say that not one report I filed, of the dozens we did in the Persian Gulf War, was cleared by the U.S. military.

Yo Media This!

"Yo, media this!" first appeared in the San Antonio Current, *March 18, 1993.*

Yo, media this!
Cult leader begs, the FBI blames, the media ducks

AS THE STANDOFF between law enforcement officials and the Branch Davidians entered its second week, the Society of Professional Journalists announced that it would assign a "Special Ethics Task Force" to see if reporters had acted ethically in covering the story.

Meanwhile, David Koresh and his followers took to hanging banners outside their compound- one of which asked for help from the Media- a move that FBI spokesman Bob Ricks said was causing the negotiation process "to be diverted." He also said that the banners, and the subsequent reporting on their messages by the media "will not hasten the release of those inside the compound." As if the FBI had at that point been extremely effective in negotiating Koresh's release and the media were just getting in the way once again.

It looks as if my petunias are going to get more fertilizer, for the FBI and the Bureau of Alcohol, Tobacco, and Firearms (ATF) are spreading it fast and thick these days.

Not that the Media aren't responsible for some high silliness in covering the story; in fact, I'd say the cult standoff is a microcosm of everything wrong with the press today.

For example, false news. How is so much of it getting reported? Is that reporters are mostly stupid and wicked fellows? No, it's that children have been sent out to cover stories instead of adults with the credentials and acumen needed to tell the rest of us what is going on.

Fox News Service, for example, sent a kid fresh from college to field produce its coverage. He panicked regularly and fumbled frequently and while a nice kid, he was definitely in over his head. As was a local television reporter who did a standup inside a portable toilet. She too was fresh to the ranks.

But, children weren't the only problem. Many broadcast journalists simply have no *real* credentials as reporters. They've spent far too much time in *front* of the tube and very little time out in the field.

This might explain the endless amount of speculation that occurred during the coverage of the Waco Cult. Every new reporter on the scene was convinced the event was soon to be over. Nearly every reporter speculated on the events going on without any hard information.

A notable exception was Paul Venema with KSAT-TV and Dale Rankin with KENS-TV. Both have healthy credentials, both are solid reporters, and while neither seem to be the glamorous stars of their respective institutions, both gave concise and meaningful reports.

But they were the exceptions to an otherwise sordid affair. The SPJ wants to investigate "ethical" decisions made by the reporters, but what they really should look at are the management decisions that led to the staffing of the cult story.

Arthur Kent, the ex-NBC reporter called an arrogant ass by many in the industry, (during the Persian Gulf War, Kent bore the moniker of "007"), may be arrogant, but he is also right about a great many things.

On a recent *Larry King Live*, he pointed out that NBC's *Dateline's* now famous debacle with explosives and a certain General Motors truck were precipitated because of NBC's demand for "ratings over quality."

Pat Clawson, a former CNN reporter, and until recently a writer for *Radio and Records* in Washington D.C. has covered the business end of television and radio stations for several years. He's convinced that at least some of the problem with television is because of events in the 1980s.

"That's when you had a lot of property being bought up by major chains. Now the notes are beginning to come due, so you've got a lot of companies cutting back wherever possible so they can pay off their notes and still make money."

Thus, according to Clawson's logic, you have news organizations hiring kids fresh out of college to cover news events because they're *cheaper* than seasoned professionals.

My agent recently informed me of a station in Birmingham, Alabama where the management in effect told all its staffers they would soon be gone in favor of kids fresh out of school. This would seem to back up Clawson's theory.

The bottom line is no one is going to care as long as ratings continue. But, it's short-sighted thinking. The desire for ratings while sacrificing quality came back to bite NBC in it's fat rump, and it has hurt many of the news organizations covering the Waco cult standoff.

Meanwhile, the morons running the FBI and the ATF have taken full advantage of the disarray in journalism and are blaming the radio and television reporters for all that has gone wrong at the Mount Carmel compound.

"You do our job and let us do ours," Ricks said at a recent news conference. Nobody I know in the press wants Ricks job. But like the military did in the Persian Gulf War, you're keeping us from doing ours.

Dallas radio station KRLD, early on, was used by Koresh and the FBI to try and end the stalemate. The FBI abused us and spit us out like used chewing gum. Now, as Koresh stretches to get his side of the story out to the press, the FBI is scandalized.

The better informed we are, the better off we are- even during a prolonged standoff with a deranged cult leader.

It's obvious the FBI has no idea what the press is all about. If the FBI knew, and if enough seasoned reporters were covering the event, I'd venture to say things would have been quite different at Mount Carmel from day one.

Oh God!

"Oh God" also appeared in the San Antonio Current at the time of the Branch Davidian siege in Waco, Texas.

"Oh God!"

"Sit tight David, I'll get back to you . . . "

THE PROBLEMS BEGAN BECAUSE the Federal Bureau of Investigation and the Bureau of Alcohol Tobacco and Firearms had not bothered to talk to the media at all since the Sunday, February 28 raid on the Mount Carmel compound of the Branch Davidian cult, 10 miles east of Waco.

That raid resulted in the death of four ATF officers and a stalemate siege with a cult that supposedly had a howitzer, 50 caliber machine guns, body armor, and grenades in its well- stocked arsenal. On Tuesday, March 2, David Koresh, who thinks he's Jesus Christ, told the FBI he'd give up if they would arrange airplay on a radio station of a 58-minute speech in which Koresh compares himself to Christ.

The FBI agreed to the broadcast, but hours after the message had been played, nothing happened. It was so silent at the compound there was concern that Koresh and his followers (who call their compound Rancho Apocalypse) had decided to join their heavenly father with the aid of some Jonestown Kool-Aid. Low and behold, late that Tuesday night buses began leaving the compound. Dallas radio station KRLD announced the siege was "apparently over," and soon there were reports of women, children, and sacrificial goats leaving the scene.

But it wasn't over. Not even close. Having bought KRLD's report,

A *Current Affatir* and two Houston broadcasts pronounced the media event to be near a successful conclusion. After many slaps on the back, reporters then began thinking of their next high-profile assignment.

Koresh though, had second thoughts. Not that he wanted to, you understand, but according to Koresh, God told him to stay put until He gave the cult leader another sign.

I thought the Bradley fighting vehicles and the tanks and the helicopters and armed FBI agents sitting outside the front door would qualify as a sign from God, but then I'm not as close to the Lord as Koresh says he is.

Finally, the next morning, the FBI decided to talk to the media and took us all to task for spreading false rumors. Excuse me? I'm not defending wild speculation, of which there was plenty that Tuesday night, but the FBI is in no position to preach to the media- nor is ATF.

The ATF staged a daylight raid on a heavily fortified compound, got their butts kicked, and then said they succumbed to superior firepower- and, oh yes, someone must have tipped off the cult.

There have been big hints leveled that it was a Waco television crew that captured the ATF slaughter on videotape that did the tipping. I spoke with Dan Mulloney, the KWTX photographer who was at the firefight, and he says he and his reporter traveled to the compound that Sunday morning because they were looking to do a story about Koresh- whose cult had been featured in a local newspaper article the day before. They *stumbled* into the raid, he told me.

"Why would we tip off the cult?" he said. "We were right in the line of gunfire too. We even helped carry some of the injured out of the way.

"This [the ATF raid] was a total disaster," retired Army colonel Charles Beckwith (the founder of the Army's elite Delta Force) said on KRLD the next day. "It showed a lack of planning and a lack of intelligence of what was going on inside the compound at the time of the raid. Losing four members of your own force and having 14 more wounded is not an acceptable loss."

But the ATF would have you believe that it was all the media's fault. So, apparently, would the FBI, which first hassled reporters at the scene, moving us first a mile and half back from the site (for our own safety, they claimed, but local residents much closer to the compound were not kept from entering their homes), then threatening to move us still further from the scene, then refusing to talk with us until the fourth day of the crisis. Meanwhile, members of media camped out in their cars, afraid of leaving the scene for fear they'd never be able to get back in. The FBI and the ATF had dozens of portable toilets brought into the compound in order to address their needs, but for four days the media did without. The FBI could see us all standing at the bottom of a hill a mile and a half away from the compound, but offered us no help.

It just shows how little the FBI thinks of the press. They don't even consider us human beings.

All this loss of life, strife, tension, and heartache was brought on by a 33-year-old ninth-grade-educated wannabe rock musician who has a messiah complex and allegedly likes to marry 14-year-old girls so he can legally rape them. The saddest part is that more than 100 fools followed this "poster child for lobotomies" into this folly believing they'd found their messiah.

The Ties That Divide

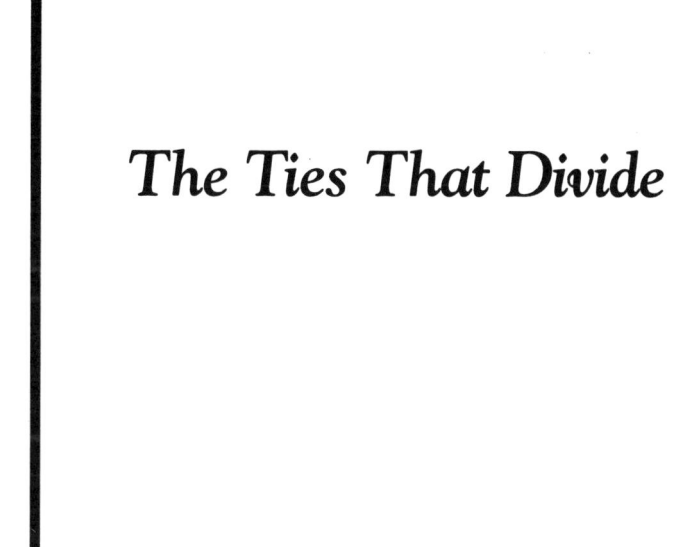

It was Will Rogers who once said that he never met a man that he didn't like. It would be nice to have a man like Will Rogers around today, if only as a counter balance against the cynics, hypocrites, hate mongers, and those humorless souls who dominate the national scene.

There is, of course, a long list of men and women in today's popular culture that are very well known who are so vastly hypocritical and so elaborately shallow that they could only play at the beginning of the Media Millennium. That's because with the joy of television and the multiplication of outlets from which to choose, today's over inflated egos can be guaranteed a national audience without ever actually having to meet anybody face to face. In the Old West, these personalities would be prostitutes, thieves, and the guys traveling through mining camps hawking their wares, magic potions, and elixirs of life. Today, they are televangelists, politicians, reporters, and anyone sitting on a television set with Regis Philbin- most especially Kathy Lee Gifford.

How else can one explain the Republican controlled House of Representatives, Senator Mitch McConnell, Newt Gingrich, Jesse Helms, Charlton Heston, Al Sharpton, and a host of other characters both loathsome and pitiable who bounce around the nation selling things for which most of us have little or no use. In the Old West, they would've been tarred, feathered, and ridden out of town on the nearest wooden rail.

Yet today, although they may be vilified, we just can't seem to get rid of them. Not to say that all of them don't have something likeable about them. In the best spirit of Will Rogers, I can point to things about all the aforementioned and plenty of others of whom I could find something to like. You've got to like Heston's perverse ability to drop the stone tablets of the Ten Commandments- which for those of you who have forgotten contains a little known edict about "Thou Shalt Not Kill"- and replace them with an automatic weapon and cheap and plentiful handguns so that first graders can cap each other at random whenever their little hearts desire. You have to also like something about the inane perversities of Newt Gingrich who, while hunting President Clinton with the vim and vigor of a Christian Missionary among the cannibals, turned out to be embroiled in his own sexual extra-marital activities.

Then again, what's not to like about a Supreme Court that decides it's okay to ban nude titty bar dancing on the vague assumption that nude dancing has harmful "secondary effects" on a community such as higher crime rates and lower property values. This is true; I can tell you from many visits to these nude bars strictly for information gathering purposes. I witnessed staggering amounts of increased crime and lower property values. The crime was cheap, watered down liquor, and my own personal property value was lowered as different contortionists separated my money from me one dollar bill at a time to the point where I had no property left.

Perhaps the NRA could jump in on this one. If you ban nude dancing then only criminals will go nude- of course no telling where they'll put their guns.

Meanwhile, back in the hallowed halls of Congress, where the mighty Sonny Bono once reigned, our elected officials will forever, it seems, be caught up in another momentous tide of indifference: banning flag burning. You have to like these guys who got elected and seem to perpetually run on a platform studded with the planks of mom, apple pie, no nude dancing, no drugs and clean flags. Somewhere in the South where a lock of hair from William Jennings Bryan is still used to cure warts, politicians are evoking all the old issues that were supposedly put to rest in the Scopes Monkey Trial. These are important issues, sure. I know there are police departments all over the country chomping at the bit to bust illegal titty bars and flag burners what with the lower violent crime rates and all.

I confess, however, that I have come to thoroughly enjoy living in the Washington D.C. area. It's much like having a front row seat to a circus. Forget Los Angeles and the movie industry. Actors are mere amateurs compared to the decadence and depravity that go on and are discussed in the most official looking conference rooms in the country. Rock music lyrics. Yep. Titty Bars. Yep. Prostitution, malfeasance, stained dresses, drugs and murder. Yep, yep, yep, you betcha and most assuredly.

Entertainers love the Washington experience, being drawn like drunken mouths to a funeral pyre, and you have to like some of the more obtuse of them. There are the Gangsta Rap stars who come and complain about the problems of racial discrimination while they sell their CD's to the poor black teenagers in the city's Southeast who can barely afford decent clothes, let alone a new CD. Then there is Pat Buchanan, an entertainer (one can hardly seriously consider him a politician any more than one can consider President Clinton virginal) so warped he tried to evoke Adolf Hitler and Gandhi in one breath. Forget the vagaries of "Compassionate Conservatism" as espoused by George W. Bush. With Buchanan we can get compassionate totalitarianism. Not since Bryan himself has the Republic been witness to such a rattling buffoon as Buchanan. He is shrill, hateful, vindictive, confusing, and as empty a soul as has ever taken the national stage.

Of course, we must not forget the tree huggers, preaching peace and love and still wearing the sandals and tie-dye from the 60s. They come to Washington to warn us about the excesses of Capitalism and progress as if they were the Unabomber himself. Then they get around to their real issue- cheap and plentiful clothes made from legal hemp. They're not hypocrites. I just love the idea of legal hemp. God made it, so why should we outlaw it, a Rastafarian once told me. I really liked him.

As it turns out, everything that was old is not only new again in Washington D.C., but you can usually find an organized group somewhere lobbying for it. The oldest and most dangerous of these issues is one that the denizens of government have trivialized and turned into political atomic bombs- the issue of race. It is this matter of that I think is of the greatest interest to me because I must confess I've been very naïve my whole life about it. For example, when the census form came to me at the beginning of the third millennium, I looked rather puzzled as I studied the different options I had for filling out the card.

There were a variety of options for telling the governmental keepers of meaningless information to what race I belonged. But after studying my multiple options for several minutes I couldn't find anything that suited me.

Finally, I took the option of writing in my answer. Down at the bottom, I check-marked the appropriate column and then wrote in "Human- Homo Sapiens." According to every science and anthropology class I ever took in high school or college that was the appropriate and accurate answer. While there have been other races of human beings, like Neanderthal and Homo Erectus, not to mention my all time favorite, Cro-Magnon, in the earth's past, there are apparently no members of these races currently wandering the globe.

We are it. One race. One people and any discussion of anything else is merely a discussion of the superficial and shallow differences that make each of us unique and make life so utterly enjoyable. So, in a very human way we've turned our distinctness, our minor yet easily recognized differences into something not beautiful, but horribly ugly. We are a shallow people, no doubt, to let such superficial differences dominate our relationships with each other in such a negative fashion. Yet discussing our different ethnic backgrounds has become almost impossible to avoid, and at the same time to merely do so is to be marked as a racist by some.

It is this ignorance of who we are and what we mean to each other that threatens to destroy the fabric of our society. Are we really so different from each other any more? Do we all not have the same opportunities to succeed? Must we have things handed to us? I was taught that a man should be evaluated by his character and not the color of his skin. Martin Luther King said it, and at the time black people in this country were afforded fewer opportunities. I'm not so sure that is the case now, and there are many who believe the pendulum has swung too far in the opposite direction. I will not comment on that as I'm not black. But I do know that everything in my own life I appreciate I have earned. Things given to me because of skin color ring hollow in my experience, whether it is because the skin is white or black.

And that is how I see the issue. It is a matter of black and white, right and wrong. Men should never be judged by the color of their skin, and to do so in this wonderful country of opportunity does us all a disservice. It is a wonderful country where illegal immigrants can wade ashore and get services and help that some legal immigrants can't get. It is a wonderful country where the huddled masses yearning to breath free can continue to speak their own language and complain about the services the government supplies them aren't enough- although, mind you, the government in their home country wouldn't lift a finger to help them- which is why they came to this country in the first place. Yes, all of this happens under the banner of human rights and the desire by the people and our government to provide a voice for everyone and tools to everyone so they may better themselves. It is a humanitarian government, and even while wrong-headed at times I find myself paraphrasing another who said this may be one screwed up country, but it's better than any other screwed up country.

So, in this country of marvelous intentions we've developed a double edge sword in dealing with race. The Civil Rights movement, white guilt, black pride, and other factors have led us to celebrate our differences. This is a very valuable thing- for after all I can only take so many rotten white-bread McDonald's fast-food restaurants before I start looking for a nice Italian Bistro. But we've also taken this idea, in some instances, a step too far. We not only celebrate our differences, but forget the common ties that bind us all together.

The English language is one of those, and forgive me if I sound as if I'm discriminating, but all I ask is not an end to affirmative action so much as a real desire to have someone on the drive-thru at a fast-food restaurant that can speak the language. My grandfather came here from Lebanon and tried very hard to fit into society by learning English. Why in the United States must I be forced to order a milkshake at Burger King in Erdu?

Of course, everyone at one time or another has been discriminated against and the reasons for discrimination are varied. Discrimination can come from insecurity, paranoia, and the desire to have someone do the really nasty slave work that no one else wants to do. Then again, in this wonderful media driven world in which we live, I've come to think that the old reasons for discrimination, prejudice, and hatred have fallen by the wayside and can now be blamed on simple boredom and ignorance in shallow and trivial minds that populate the country from coast to coast.

The actions of prejudice and discrimination have come handed down from generation to generation like family heirlooms. And like the moldy old clock that never worked but is valued because some ancestor owned it, so, too, has prejudice and discrimination been given to the future. Sadly, children who learn of hatred and intolerance from their parents, who in turn had learned it from their parents ad nauseam, are trapped into a learned behavior and seem to have no way out, let alone being able to grasp they need one.

Indeed, this is where the boredom factors in. Life at the beginning of this millennium, even for many of the poorest residents, has become boring. We don't challenge ourselves intellectually. We play Nintendo and watch television. We don't learn new crafts and go to schools to advance ourselves. We see ourselves as victims who are owed something from someone- anyone else. Life has become so boring for many people that they must invent challenges to overcome. Conveniently there are minorities, homosexuals, and women on which to blame your boredom and discontent. From your parents you've learned all you need is to blame others for your misfortune and make yourself a pitiable victim. For many who fall into such a trap they simply cannot grasp that their prejudice is a learned behavior because they've never thought outside their own little box.

"United We Stand, Divided We Fall" is the motto of the state of Kentucky and a lesson we should all learn from our past- the American Revolution. Thirteen colonies, as different as a New Yorker and a Georgian are today found they had more in common with each other and banded together to expel the English Crown. Must we always have an enemy to bind us together? Can we not see that our ties are deeper than that?

I've not been immune to the hurtful insults that come from discrimination. Growing up in the South with a last name of Karem gave me an opportunity and insight that everyone should be exposed to at least once in their life. To begin with, no one could ever pronounce my last name, although it seems quite easy. It is pronounced "Care-Um." Not hard, but to this day I'm always called Kareem as in Abdul Jabbar. Thus growing up in Louisville, Kentucky I was Brian "Care-Eem" the "Aaa-Rab" as in the song "Ahab the Arab." Being dark complected and with dark hair I was also routinely referred to as "towel head," "rag head," "Sand Nigger," and when no one was quite sure what ethnicity I belonged to I was alternately called "Kike," "Wop,"

"Jew," "Spic," and my all time favorite, "Greaser," which I thought was someone who worked the oil and lube rack at the local gas station until I was told otherwise.

There was a recalcitrant group of reprobates in my neighborhood of dubious lineage (I'm still not convinced some Neanderthal did not survive in some various form or fashion and now have mutated into what H.L. Mencken called "Boobus Americanus"). These reprobates spat at me while I rode my bike on several occasions, threatened to beat me up whenever it suited them, and in between driving loud, lousy cars, and stealing lawn and garden equipment from the sheds of everyone in the neighborhood, they made it a point to pick on the neighborhood "Sand Nigger."

Despite these experiences, which were very demeaning- after all it isn't fun to wipe someone else's mucous from your face- I didn't grow up thinking I was a victim because of my ethnicity or that I belonged to a class of people who were owed special favors or privileges from the government. The insults hurt, but my father taught me that they came from ignorant people and I should ignore them. Ethnicity, I was taught was something we all had, but it wasn't a yardstick by which I was to measure anyone. No single particular ethnicity was superior to another. Myself, I barely noticed ethnicity as it didn't factor into my daily life. When you're on the playground no one cares what color you are as long as you can kick, hit, and catch. I wasn't one of the last picked when we divided up the teams because my name was Karem. I was among the last because I spent, in my youth, more time playing chess and studying science than kicking a kickball- something I quickly tried to rectify when I realized that girls liked athletes.

I even remember a brief time when I believe there was a chance for this country to eliminate the inherent hatred of ethnic discrimination. It was the mid to late 70s. *Shaft* was popular with black and white audiences where I grew up. I listened to Richard Pryor, not because he cussed, but because when he talked about his father it reminded me of my own Dad- a strict, but loving authoritarian. That Richard grew up near a whorehouse, well, that was just icing on the cake.

Elsewhere, we all listened to Sly and the Family Stone, Santana, The Rolling Stones, and wore horribly gauche clothing with neckties wide enough to count as bibs. Platform heels, wedgies, earth shoes, and flared jeans where commonly seen on people of every color and ethnicity. In short, no one had any taste in clothing and after "Glam Rock" and "Disco" became popular it was obvious everyone lost whatever taste we had in music.

I remember this time in my teens as very strange. It started out with court ordered desegregation of the Jefferson County public schools. While there were riots, demonstrations and a hell raised the likes of which I hadn't seen before, after a few weeks of school, it all seemed to die away. Forced integration worked for many because it exposed us to people and ways of thinking and realities we'd never before had experienced. Life did not end when school busing came to Louisville despite the rednecks' claims to the contrary.

In my neighborhood, it didn't affect life much. My father, who'd been exposed to the same type of ethnic insults I had was a football coach, and routinely kids of all color and ethnicity came over to my house to play after football practice until their parents could come pick them up. My father never seemed to care what color anyone was, and no one else I hung around with ever seemed to notice unless color was used as was weight, hair color and eye color in describing someone. It was the 70s, and we all seemed to be making great strides in getting along.

By the time I left my idyllic youth and went to college, Ronald Reagan and then George Bush took over the office of the Presidency, and the "Me" Generation had come into power. Greed, Avarice, and Lust replaced Harmony and Tolerance. The rich got richer, the poor got a lot poorer, and the best way the rich had to keep everyone ignorant of this was to separate the rest of us by race. White people have a lot more in common with black people than rich people Warren Beatty said in *Bulworth*. Nothing rings truer.

The problems of ethnic tolerance, prejudice, and hatred are deep-seeded problems in this country. There is no denying it and no denying that some white people feel as discriminated against as blacks do. There is no denying that black people feel put upon and have been pushed down for hundreds of years. Others of different ethnicity, even those of other sexual preferences, all feel they've been culled from the herd and marked for derision. In fact, I strongly suspect if you separate everyone who claims to be a victim from the whole of the U.S. population there will be many groups of victims and no one left in the middle. But I also suspect whites and blacks alike use discrimination as a tool, a red herring, and a way to stir up the pot and foment anarchy. Can I get an "Amen" or perhaps a "Duh?"

Yet, while this notion seems a no-brainer to me, it seems to escape those seduced by the cry to arms and a shout for intolerance. Once, while a young reporter in Laredo, Texas our President talked about the Sandinistas and other horrifying people being just a mere day's march from the Texas-Mexican border. A few days later, some guys in white, pointy hats showed up to volunteer to man the border to help the Border Patrol stem the tide of nastiness that was sure to come swarming over the border at any minute from points South.

Ten members of the Ku Klux Klan showed up before television cameras and reporters telling us they each represented a thousand members of the KKK and that those 10,000 would be down to defend the country against the scourge of "Our Brown Brothers" to the South, should anyone get any idea of invading the United States. Unfortunately for them, about a hundred members of the League of United Latin American Citizens, or LULAC showed up to protest the KKK protest. The LULAC protestors didn't claim to represent anyone but themselves, but it was very effective. Obviously the KKK forgot that Laredo's population is about 95 percent Hispanic Catholics and it didn't matter if the KKK's legion of ten who showed up represented a mythical 10,000. One hundred pissed off Hispanic Catholics versus 10 pointy-head morons don't add up to much of a victory for the KKK, so the pointy white heads fled- just ahead of the tar, feathers, and rail I imagine.

I remember another time when I was confronted by similar ethnic stupidity. I was wearing an Al Sharpton for Senate t-shirt to one of my children's soccer games when he was very young. It distressed an older woman to no end. I'd bought the shirt while covering a Sharpton rally when I did a piece on the senate race that included Sharpton and Geraldine Ferraro. "How can you wear that in public?" The woman asked me. "That man is an abomination."

I looked at my t-shirt and then at the woman. "Well, first I put my head through it and then my left and finally my right arm. It's how I wear most of my t-shirts."

True to the spirit of Will Rogers, I like Al Sharpton although I know many who don't. An acerbic, bombastic man, he moves through a crowd like a human tugboat. Once during a campaign fundraiser in Brooklyn, Al got me. Appearing on a raised staged in a large room with Spike Lee and other notables in the community, Al made his pitch for money. The big double doors in the back of the room slowly closed, trapping hundreds of people inside the ballroom.

"Now, those people in the media," Al said pointing directly at me and my camera crew from *Broadcast New York*, "say that only the poor black people are behind me. Now's your chance to show them that the rich black people are supporting me too."

With that said, two men toting wicker baskets walked through the crowd. The implication was obvious. If you wanted out of the room you had to pay. It resembled a Sunday at church as everyone dressed up in their finest dumped checks of undetermined amounts into the wicker baskets. But Al was happy. Many of the donors looked at the only tan boy in the room (me) with derision. But hey, I didn't tell them they had to pay. Al did.

Afterwards, I told him it was obvious to me that he meant to make me uncomfortable as I was the only white guy in the audience. He smiled and then laughed, and I couldn't help but laugh, too. Then we went on to another topic of discussion as I continued to interview him. At one point in time he stopped me and told me I didn't understand the point he was trying to make because my forefathers had owned his forefathers.

"My forefathers didn't own shit," I told him. "That's why they came to this country at the beginning of the 20th Century. We were the only Catholics in a country overrun with Moslems."

He looked at me and smiled again. Then he laughed. "Well, you get my point," he said laughing. Indeed, I did, and I couldn't help but think about playing poker with Al Sharpton. Might be fun. Al may be full of bombast, but at least he knows it. He also knows how to laugh.

I think that ability would help us all out a bit. Life is too serious to be taken so seriously someone once said. To quote Rodney King, "Can't we all just get along?"

It's time we all stopped seeing ourselves as victims and took a little responsibility for our own lives. It has to start with liking ourselves enough to like other people too. It sounds naïve, but then again I've always been naïve when it comes to this stuff for I find I have too much in common with too many people to ever be able to look down upon any group of people any where just because they think differently than I do, dress differently, look differently or act differently. Variety is the spice of life another cliché tells us. How true. I enjoy the spice an awful lot, and I suspect there are many who are not too bored, afraid, or ignorant of life to feel the same thing.

I wish I was more like Will Rogers. His ancestry included the American Indian (don't even get me started on Native American. I was born here. That makes me a Native American). But Will Rogers never forgot his roots and never sowed the seeds of hatred in trying to stand up for who and what he was. He often joked that his family didn't come over on the Mayflower, but they met those in the boat when they came ashore. Will had a sense of humor.

Wish he were around now.

My, My, Honey, But You Have a Fine . . .

OF THE MANY POLITICIANS on the national and local stage it's been my privilege to spend time with during the last 20 years, the Texas politicians stand out in my mind as the most colorful. Whether it be Phil Gramm, Lloyd Doggett, R.C Centeno, Ann Richards, Henry Cisneros or a host of other known and unknowns, there is something about a Texas politician which makes he or she as easy to spot and appreciate as a Texas Bluebonnet in a field of common daisies.

If, for example, it is taken as a truism that everything is bigger in Texas, then the politicians follow suit. When corrupt they are openly and horribly so. When they are noble, they are almost angelic. When angry they are petulant and mean, and when they make mistakes they do so in such a manner that makes for the best television and newspaper copy. Even the best of Texas politicians are a little rough around some edges and some more than others. But their foibles are refreshing compared to the staid and boxed politics of other regions. The politicians in Texas, for a lack of a better term, just seem more human.

The man who embodies this gestalt more than any other man or woman to me is a man who is unknown outside of San Antonio, Texas. He was a sheriff for about eight years, and when he tried to step up from local politics to state politics by helping out a member of his party who was running for Governor of the Lone Star State, he was greeted with jeers, cat calls, and laughter. People in San Antonio, a city by and large of many unrefined and earthy types, also routinely dismissed him as a rube and a bumpkin. In many ways, he was. But, he was also much more.

His name is Harlon Copeland. As a sheriff he was as distinct as he was colorful. With his big barrel-chest he was as apt to wear a belt buckle the size of his white-haired head as he was to wear the ubiquitous Texas cowboy boots. Most of the members of the press in San Antonio in the late 80s and early 90s despised him and cursed him as crude and inerudite. True to the man's spirit, he didn't give a crap in hell about what reporters thought of him. He had a monumental ego, and his attitude of disdain was not exclusively for reporters, either. He ruled his department with an iron fist, fought often with other politicians, and his staff lived in fear of him because it was often said that Harlon's rules on Monday didn't necessarily apply on Tuesday. He never seemed to care. Naturally, I got along great with him.

He was the sheriff who referred to a riot in his jail as a "Butt Kickin' contest, and we won." He asked then gubernatorial candidate Ann Richards if she had ever "Done drugs," and tried to investigate her for it. True to his image, Harlon also was not above letting everyone know that he was the "highest damn law enforcement officer in the county" whenever the San Antonio Police tried to muscle him- which they did often because the more urbane police department saw the smaller sheriff's department as a gang of rowdies. But Harlon, also known as "High Noon Copeland," and whose jail was known as either the "Harlon Hilton" or the "Copeland Cabana," never flinched from criticism and routinely gave as good as he got.

He cultivated his bumpkin image, right down to campaigning on a fire truck and professing to be a proud redneck. He loved old cars and even had a taste for classical music, which he didn't let too many people know about.

He was a Republican, but only on paper, because I know he hired many Democrats in his sheriff's office, and he had a lot of common sense and cared a lot for your average taxpayer- something I've found usually lacking in Republicans of all ilks. During the late 80s as gang violence, some of it imported from Los Angeles, sprang up all over San Antonio, the local police department, via their mouthpiece Paul Buske was busy telling everyone there was no gang problem in the city. Harlon took the exact opposite tactic and formed the county's first, and ultimately best, gang unit and went after the gangs. "I got the biggest gang in Bexar County," Harlon was fond of saying. Harlon would never have played any where else in the country, but he was right at home in San Antonio and for years provided me with exclusive interviews and allowed me to ride along with his narcotics unit as they busted meth labs, coke dealers, and the assorted heroin dealers.

He also made a very big deal out of cleaning up dozens of massage parlors that dotted the outskirts of San Antonio. Once, while he rode with his deputies on a raid, he walked into a massage parlor, and, recognizing a well-known businessman inside, clearly called out the man's name as the cameras were rolling. "What are you doin' in here?" Harlon asked. "You'd better get home before I tell on you." Of course he already had.

Harlon got a kick out of the massage parlor raids, and, once while raiding a massage parlor that also sold sexually explicit toys, he grabbed a large flesh colored cone and asked one of his deputies what it was for. The deputy, cognizant of the cameras, walked over to Harlon and whispered in Harlon's ear. Harlon turned and looking out to the cameras said in a full, booming voice, "You mean they stick this up their butts?"

Harlon, though, was no fool, and I say in all sincerity that the man never once lied to me in all the years I knew him. He would tell me if something was none of my business, or he just wouldn't answer a question, but never did I catch him lying to me. That can't be said for all politicians, and it is why Harlon rides so high in my memory.

There is another Texas politician who also rates high on my scale, and that's because he was the exact opposite of Harlon, and yet he also came from San Antonio. Henry Cisneros is perhaps one of the most urbane, witty, and ultimately tragic politicians I've ever known. I admire him a great deal and remember when I first met him during the early to mid 80s. Henry was just bursting on the San Antonio scene, and he was the answer to every Hispanic's prayer. Where many Hispanic politicians before Henry were routinely course and sometimes crude, Henry was erudite and suavely smooth. He was well educated, handsome, well-dressed, and could talk the language of the barrio and the boardroom. In South Texas, and I mean deep South Texas, down around Laredo for example, Henry was as close to the second coming of Christ in the mid 80s as a living man could get.

In many Hispanic/Catholic homes there were usually three very prominent pictures on display in the home at that time. There was Jesus, the Virgin Mary, and a portrait of John Kennedy. You could travel through the nicest and the poorest homes in the area and be virtually guaranteed of spotting those three pictures- usually hanging right next to each other in the living room. Enter Henry Cisneros and suddenly there are four pictures hanging on the wall in your average South Texas home. Henry was thought of very highly in South Texas at that time, universally loved and admired, but like Icarus and Daedalus, Henry flew too close to the sun and got burned.

It happened, some said, because of Henry's upbringing. Dave Rodrick, an MSNBC producer and former city hall reporter at KMOL-TV in San Antonio blamed Henry's youth. Henry apparently had been a book worm and didn't get the attention of the ladies in high school, and Dave often speculated at KMOL that perhaps Henry was trying to make up for lost time as an adult. Certainly his reputation as a lady's man was well known. Even before anyone ever printed a word about Henry's extra-marital affair with then Linda Medlar, I was queried by my barber as to whether or not it was true that the famous and well-loved Catholic mayor of San Antonio was stepping out on his wife. It was, in fact, the worst kept secret in town.

Cisneros and his love-life had been the talk of newsrooms for many months at the time. But, in those days before the *National Enquirer* mentality took over journalism and eons before a President spread his seed on some intern's dress, nobody much cared. I sure didn't. Since Cisneros never made an issue of his love-life, and because he continued to do a fairly credible job as Mayor, no one ever wrote about his peccadilloes. He had, in fact, told everyone it was his private business, and for a while reporters- believe it or not- respected that.

But a reporter can respect something for only so long. It seems an inherently iconoclastic domain, so soon, naturally, the story made both of the daily newspapers: the now defunct *San Antonio Light* and the *San Antonio Express-News*. Then the radio and television stations waded into it. I remember standing on the lawn of Henry's house as he talked to dozens of reporters, holding press conferences in both English and Spanish. I could never get over that. Henry was so cordial and polite even as he aired his dirtiest and most personally humiliating laundry. The man was more than a gentleman; he was a Catholic boy wracked with guilt. I've seen the type many times- hell, I've even been that type on an occasion or two. But, there was no denying the class with which Henry handled himself that day when the world found out he was stepping out on his wife. I marvel at his ability to continue doing so. The story, which we thought at the time would die within a few weeks has taken on a life of its own of course.

In 1992, Henry joined the Clinton team and that's when it really got ugly. His mistress (now thankfully ex-mistress) began tape recording conversations with him, and Henry made colossally ridiculous admissions on tape. He left the administration and the FBI dogged him and charged him. Other than proving what an unbelievable bitch Henry's former mistress is, I've never been completely sure of why they hunted him so.

Through it all, for the last 12 years Henry has had to live with his mistake hanging over him like a money and emotion sucking vulture. Besides his ex-mistress, he's also had to contend with the public recrimination, court appearances, and the price of attorneys. He's managed to raise a family which includes raising a son who had a potentially fatal birth defect. That he's managed to do all that he's done without going postal is a good indication of just what type of man he is. He'd make one hell of a President, but he won't ever get the chance, and it is the country's loss, not his.

Speaking of the public's loss, it is a shame more people never got to know the Commissioner's Court from Webb County Texas in the early and mid 80s. A bigger band of incompetents and bunglers were never assembled in one place at one time. There was J.R. Esparza who thought of himself as an interior decorator and used County money to tear up the yard outside of the County Courthouse, and after ridding the four small patches of ground of their lawns, he replanted the areas with gardens that were supposed to showcase the "South Texas flavor" of Laredo and Webb County. Webb County, being where it was, is an arid patch of land more reminiscent of a desert than anything else. There was, of course, no grass nor hardly a plant at all in the garden. There was a lot of dry ground, a broken wagon wheel, a Longhorn skull, a broken split rail fence, and several weeds planted in the yard. It spawned a lot of laughs as it looked more like a South Texas ranch after years of drought than any kind of garden. J.R. fumed when people got upset about it and twirled his handlebar mustache furiously in protest as if he were some South Texas version of Snideley Whiplash.

Also present in that Commissioner's Court was a sheriff who was rumored to have been shot in his ass by the jealous husband of his mistress as the sheriff climbed out of his mistress's second story bedroom window. I saw the sheriff walking with a cane but was never able to confirm the shooting.

Then there was R.C. Centeno. He was a County Commissioner who had several "Colonias" in his jurisdiction. Nothing ever seemed to be done about the illegal and slum-ridden subdivisions which had few or, in one case, no paved roads, no electricity, and no running water. The city fumed about the problem, yet no one in the county could ever understand why Centeno didn't do more to help his poorer constituents. The fact that Centeno Grocery, situated on Centeno Lane in one of the Colonias, run by Centeno's daughter who later also became a County Commissioner after her father died, had nothing to do with Centeno's lack of determination we were all assured.

Other Texas politicians stand out in my mind as well. Lloyd Bentsen's withering insult to Dan Quayle was perhaps his best known quip on a national level, but in Texas he was often known to be of keen insight and quick wit. Then there was Attorney General Jim Mattox who wanted to become governor, and to prove he had the stomach to put death row inmates to the needle he attended every execution he could while in office- which is a considerable amount in Texas where they try to put down at least one or two a week- sometimes one or two a day if they can schedule them properly.

Clayton Williams, the Republican gubernatorial candidate that Harlon Copeland tried to help, was another character of Texas size. He was the man who quipped that if you're getting raped you might as well sit back, relax and enjoy it. No one was surprised when Ann Richards, a woman whose hair was so white that television photographers used to get a "white balance" off her hair, won the election. Ann's election was seen as a major victory for women and liberals, and I remember all too well her first news conference after her election.

It was a cluster-fuck of biblical proportions, at least that's what one reporter said as we all stood outside the Governor's office in Austin waiting for Ann to show up. Naturally bored with waiting, reporters and photographers began discussing the difference between a "cluster fuck," a "pig fuck," and just normal gridlock. It was decided that gridlock was the presence of between five and 10 television cameras with the necessary television, print, and radio reporters thrown in. Anything under that number was just considered a small pig fuck or regular news conference- take your pick.

The dozens of reporters and photographers who made up the entourage outside of the state offices got into a very deep and hearty discussion about the matter- some even taking notes as if the matter would be written about in the next edition of a journalism college textbook. Finally, it was decided that the presence of 10-15 television cameras along with the necessary photographers, reporters, technicians and radio and print reporters constituted the well respected and awe inspiring "cluster fuck."

Anything over 15 television cameras constituted a major cataclysmic event and would there after be entitled a "goat fuck." Quickly, the reporters counted the television cameras and alas and alack there were but 14 cameras present. Then, suddenly out of the office building emerged the newly elected governor of the Great State of Texas, Ann Richards, along with not one but two television cameras representing a *60 Minutes* crew.

"We have Goat! We have Goat!" went up the cry from at least two of the loudest reporters in the bunch. There was much laughter and huzzahs all around- except from the newly elected governor who mistakenly got the impression we were all talking about her. I don't think she ever truly forgave me for that- and Ann Richards could hold a grudge.

Finally, in the pantheon of unforgettable politicians there is a man who is more, and at the same time less, than a politician. Although he isn't from Texas, he is from Louisiana and grew up not too far from the Texas border, at least if you judge distances the way they do in Texas. He routinely calls himself a "Coon Ass" which I wasn't sure quite how to take when I first met him, but later came to like him and respect him quite a bit, although I'm not sure if I'll ever be comfortable calling anyone, let alone James Carville, a "Coon Ass."

Carville has never held public office and swears he's too weird to do so. "I'm like Uranium 235," he has said on numerous occasions. "I'm not quite stable."

I met him in 1996 when *Playboy* paid me to interview him. It was a raucous ride that took me on a cross-country trip and through the heart of the most bizarre spectacles in Hollywood. James was on his way to Memphis, Tennessee, for a three-day shoot on the movie *The*

People Vs. Larry Flynt, and we began the interview in between takes on the movie. James seemed slightly uncomfortable at first with the Hollywood people with whom he was working and invited me to have dinner with him one night as he dined with the likes of Courtney Love, Milos Forman, and, of course, Larry Flynt.

James was fascinated by Flynt, and I listened and occasionally joined in as the pair discussed politics, corruption, drugs, movies, and everything else under the sun. A few minutes later, a woman I didn't recognize walked up to Flynt and began talking to him as Carville watched. James seemed slightly upset that the woman had barged in on their conversation and he turned to me and said, "These damn Hollywood types can be rude, Brian."

I had to turn to listen to him because Milos Forman, who was sitting next to me, was busy giving me a dissertation on the Universe. Forman had recently read a *Time* or *Newsweek* article which had said something to the effect that there were 12 billion galaxies in the Universe. Fascinated by that statistic, Forman couldn't stop talking about it. "Who counted all of those galaxies, dear boy?" he asked.

I didn't know and stopped to turn to Carville. Then I looked at the woman who had interrupted his conversation with Flynt. She had dark hair, dark, dirty looking fingernails and a complexion like gray wax. I figured her for an addle-brained coke or heroin freak who saw Flynt and was trying to con her way into the pages of *Hustler*. I was close. It was Courtney Love.

Carville didn't seem to want to have much to do with Love, or Woody Harrelson or any of the other so-called "stars" on the set. He liked Flynt and Forman. Carville also gravitated to some of the people who recognized him at the bar and wanted to strike up conversations with him. He always seemed most comfortable with those who couldn't do anything for him. He once said he thought of himself as kind of like a piano player in a whorehouse. But there is little doubt he sold himself short.

Republicans, of course, can't stand him. And I never could figure out why or what drove him into the arms of Mary Matalin, a woman as strident in her desire to trumpet the Republican cause as James is to sound the Democratic horn. On the other hand, I wasn't immediately sure what would drive Mary Matalin, a strong-willed, intelligent and attractive woman into the arms of a man who looked like a bull dog, and called himself a "Coon Ass" either.

After three days together, I found out. We finished most of the *Playboy* interview on Larry Flynt's private jet, which Flynt had supplied to fly James to Portland, Oregon. Carville had agreed to stay for an extra day of shooting in Memphis only on the condition he could get to Portland by Valentine's Day to meet his wife and make a scheduled public appearance. The jet was rounded up and offered to meet Carville's needs.

Upon stepping off the plane and driving into downtown Portland, Carville saw his wife for the first time in nearly a week. The glee was apparent on his face. Standing in front of him was Mary Matalin looking stunning in a red, flowing chiffon gown. "My, my honey, but you have a fine figure," James said, although he didn't say "figure." He said something else. "You better say figure for that magazine of yours," he cautioned me. "I don't want my daughter growing up knowing the hound that I am."

He smiled and then turned his attention back to his wife. In good nature she chided James about his time in Memphis. She seemed particularly interested in teasing him about wanting to engage in intimate relations with Courtney Love. "Admit it, you liked her. You wanted her," she teased.

James vociferously denied the allegations. Then he turned to me and said, "Brian if you had the choice of fuckin' Larry Flynt or fuckin' Courtney Love, who would you fuck?"

"Gee that's a tough one," I said, trying to appear like I was giving it some serious thought. "But I guess I'd have to go with Larry Flynt."

He smiled and turned back to Mary. "See, I told you she was a nasty, skanky ho.'"

I marveled at the differences between Mary and James. Mary had prepared detailed notes for her speech that night and reviewed them in James' presence while doing her makeup back stage. James had no notes of course, but turned to me and asked if I had a piece of paper and a pen he could borrow to jot down some ideas. I handed him my reporter's notebook and a pen. He doodled a bit and wrote down a couple of lines and that was it.

On stage, they were both impressive. Both are passionate, concerned, and bright people who care about each other as much as they do about the future of the country. Whether you agree or disagree with either of them it is refreshing in such a jaded age to meet and know people who honestly believe in what they are doing. For those who continue to flirt with the naïveté of idealism, neither James nor his wife will let you down.

Of course, the Genifer Flowers affair was very much in the spotlight in those days before Monica Lewinsky and her ugly dress. Someone in the audience, enamored at how much James and Mary seemed to enjoy each other's company while arguing so passionately against one another in the political arena, asked them if they went home and argued about Genifer Flowers.

At this, James screwed up his face into something resembling a constipated hog.

"Genifa' Flowas'? Genifa' Flowas?" James said. "Now you take a look at my wife. If you were married to something as fine as that would you go home and talk about Genifa' Flowas'?"

The audience responded with a hearty laugh and Mary smiled.

Other politicians have also seared their way into memory for deeds great and small. I'll never forget Gary Hart forlornly traveling the Iowa countryside after his sexual exploits came to light. He appeared at one point at a coffee brunch where there couldn't have been more than six old women in attendance and even fewer reporters and photographers. By the time he waded through hip deep mud on a pig farm to one or two reporters and an obviously unhappy pig, it was easy enough to see that Gary Hart was done. He looked as unhappy as the pig.

Jesse Jackson never ceases to amaze me in his ability to appeal to people who otherwise would have nothing to do with him. In Iowa I once watched him embrace a man with a confederate flag on his hat and the man proclaimed, "Iowa loves you, Jesse."

The first time I covered President Bill Clinton was while Clinton was running for his first term. He appeared down in Texas with the other Democratic candidates and looked like the longest of long shots. Coming in at the very end of the function, my photographer and I decided to follow Clinton to his next event, a private affair where there were no media invited. I anticipated trouble, but Clinton was very adept, as most good politicians are, at changing gears to enjoy the free media.

He asked me whom I worked for, what questions I was interested in asking, then taking a moment, he plunged right in. He stood in a dark suit, with no handlers, but, like the best stand-up comedian, he could improvise. He spoke cogently on some very Texas-specific issues, even mentioning the Edwards Aquifer (The major source of San Antonio drinking water) to make a point about water pollution.

The next time I saw him he was wailing on a saxophone at the Arkansas Ball during the inaugural festivities in 1992.

Finally, no discussion of politicians can be complete without mentioning the hundreds or thousands of politicians who do the right thing every day. Often they are unnamed and unsung, but they are the school board members who quietly put down efforts to burn and ban literature like *A Catcher in the Rye*. They are the city aldermen and city council members who successfully fight the rampant stupidity that often overwhelms them from every angle.

They are like my grandfather, a former judge who saw politics as a noble profession and a way to help rather than hurt people. There are still many, like David and Pete Karem, a state senator and former judge respectfully from Louisville, Kentucky; two relatives who got into politics for the right reasons and who avoid going with the superficial flow of public opinion to be real leaders. They stick by their guns and they do what's right. Politics has always attracted men of such caliber, but the problem is keeping them. We never keep the best for very long it seems, for who wants to suffer the degradation we foist upon politicians on a daily basis?

It is true we get the government we deserve. Our politicians are often a reflection of the best and the worst we have in this country. But the derision and disgust we have and teach our children to have for politicians will ensure that future generations have nothing but the worst of the lot holding public office.

Somehow, we have to change all of that.

Electing Henry Cisneros to a high office would be a great way to start, but don't look for Henry to run any time soon.

Dead Bodies and Pancake Makeup

WHAT IS BIZARRE? What events every day life can one label as being "once in a lifetime" and where can you sell them? For those with the answer please feel free to fill out the coupon at the end of this article and send it with your cash, check, or credit card number to any television station in the country for usually television news will be obliged to take on the strange, bizarre and truly unique- unless of course it has to do with Woody Allen or any of the denizens of Long Island. They've long ago become passé.

But television does have a voracious appetite for the weird and off the wall. How else to explain Roseanne, Ellen, Drew Carey, Fox Television, and Dan Rather. The problem, of course, is that in the world of television news-entertainment, the bizarre becomes the common place, and the truly unique ends up as a thirty second VO read by well groomed anchors with permanent eyeliner tattooed on their eyelids.

Take for example the subject of crime. Crime is an indispensable commodity in the modern newsroom. In television news, a lengthy hostage situation, court room drama, the odd shooting, and arson fire can provide numerous opportunities for "great video" which may or may not include video of grieving relatives, body bags, roaring fires, and crime scene tape. If the crime is with a famous or infamous celebrity, á la O.J. Simpson, Tonya Harding or any rapper/singer named Tupac, well, so much the better. The viewer gets the sense, by seeing these pictures, that something newsworthy happened somewhere to someone else, and, thank God, it wasn't the disassociated viewer who's gaining a voyeuristic thrill watching murder and mayhem on the small screen.

The television producer is also pleasantly sated by crime for he or she gets to fill a minute-and-a-half to a two-minute hole in their news program and can walk away a happy camper. The anchor at the station also benefits from crime reporting. Besides justifying their exorbitant salary by keeping their wide, spreading butts firmly glued to the anchor chair, the anchor usually gets to talk dramatically about ongoing events of which they are only vaguely aware, and, at the same time, they get themselves some good tape to slap on their resume which they will use to get them to the next biggest market- or which they can use to justify an even larger salary.

It is the reporter and the photographer at the scene of these crimes that usually take the greatest risks and reap the smallest rewards. The same can be said of covering natural disasters as well. Covering hurricanes and tornadoes, it is the reporter and photographer who lash themselves to telephone poles to get the "great video" and extraordinary reports for their networks, stations, and newspapers. It is the anchor, or the city editor at the newspaper who gets to set back and pontificate on the effort.

There is a certain amount of crime beat reporting that is much like covering a natural disaster as well. The event is usually quickly breaking, there is sometimes little time to consult with the organizational hierarchy, and you'd better be sure you don't "miss" anything important that happens. Thus, crime beat reporters become adrenalin junkies, anxious to gather everything, miss nothing and make their daily deadlines- of which there may be three or four. Crack addicts may experience a high similar to that of the crime beat reporter in larger markets, but the high doesn't last as long, and it isn't anywhere near as fun. A good crime beat reporter can be recognized by his or her fingernails, usually bitten to the nubs, the beady eyes furtively darting around from person to person as if expecting and half hoping for something to happen right in front of them, and their constant need to have a portable telephone nearby.

Crime beat reporters who've been at it awhile can further be identified by their ability to only remember parts of towns or entire cities or states by the horrific crimes they've covered there. If one is to ask a veteran crime beat reporter how to get to Line St., for example, don't be surprised to hear something like, "Oh, yeah. Line Street. You go down Gardiner Lane past where that triple murder occurred last summer, make a left at the crack house where they busted those dopers and found the mummified bodies, and then go for two blocks until you come to Canyon Lake where they found the floaters, then make a left and go for two miles until you get to the site of that warehouse that burned down and killed 27 people two years ago. That's Line Street."

I've seen reporters whose entire recollection of the state of Florida amounts to, "Oh yeah, great state. They caught a serial killer there and that doctor who was raping and robbing his patients. Great place to vacation. Stayed at a hotel where there was an axe-murderer." To them the bizarre has become the mundane. You can, after all, only cover so many stories that begin with "So this guy killed his wife with a mail box post," before your eyes glaze over and you start thinking about what's for lunch. After so long covering crime, your senses are rubbed numb and raw. One simply loses the ability to tell any longer what is bizarre and what is not. Is it bizarre to see a dead, naked man lying in the middle of a deserted road in Northwestern Bexar County Texas? No. That was almost common place near San Antonio. Well, then was it bizarre to see a large grackle, those huge black birds, perched on the man carefully devouring the dead man's flesh? Perhaps if it was the man's penis? Is it strange to cover a beheading? Perhaps two?

Or is it bizarre to see a gang member shot in the head, and supposedly dead, rise from the crime scene and swear vengeance on those who shot him. If that seems surreal, then how about a car accident victim crushed from the waist down, pinned between a truck and a van who knows he's dying ask to have the cops bring his wife to him so he can see her before he dies?

If that seems mundane, then there is always the case of the man and the chicken. In San Antonio, there was a small closet converted into an office that served as the place for crime beat reporters to sit and wait mostly, but occasionally sift through crime reports or write stories. On the wall of the office, for many years, was a police report filled out in all sincerity by a police officer who happened upon a man who was presumed to have violated a chicken.

The officer observed feathers around the man's pants and a very nervous looking chicken on the ground next to the man.

"What did you do to that chicken?" the officer asked.

"What chicken?" The man replied.

Obviously the escape for many reporters from the horrors of crime becomes a macabre sense of humor. For example, when a man in San Antonio blew off his own head with a stick of dynamite he was trying to ram into a pipe, the cops and the reporters had a field day with stupid criminal jokes. One cop even picked up a piece of the skull and approached his sergeant. "You want pepperoni with it boss?" the cop asked.

The truth is the proximity to death and destruction on a daily basis taints the best of individuals, warping them beyond the normal reaches of most civilization. Take for example "Kid Death," a reporter at one of the newspapers in San Antonio in the late 80's. Tom Edwards, a bright man, balding with a beard and perpetually carrying a pipe was one of the most devoted and highly regarded crime reporters in San Antonio. One morning, while covering what eventually came to be a triple murder and suicide involving lesbian lovers on the city's northside, Tom showed up at the scene of the crime at perhaps 7 a.m. munching on a big hamburger and fries. Just a few feet away was a huge puddle of blood.

"That's brain blood," Tom said to his *San Antonio Light* cohort, a stout man who looked and acted like John Belushi.

"How do you know that?" His cohort said.

Chomp. Tom took a big bite of his sandwich and downed it with some Coca-Cola.

"See it's all gelatinous. That's how you know it's brain blood."

Chomp. The Belushi look alike, with his own sandwich, heartily agreed and bit down into his cuisine.

Truth is there has to be some sense of humor, gallows or otherwise, developed if you want to cover crime for any length of time. In the four years and assorted months I covered crime in San Antonio I came to see several hundred dead people in every state of disarray in which a human body can find itself. I remember each one of them. There were the floaters, drowning victims who after a few days in the water begin to resemble boiled chicken. The bodies, usually completely drained of blood it seemed, flaked apart as police tried to fish them into boats. There are the shooting victims and the decayed corpses-sometimes found days or weeks after their death. There were burn victims, mutilated corpses, and the occasional accident victim that looked for all the world like ground beef wearing blue jeans.

How bad it gets depends on how close you want to get to the bone. Once while doing a special on the Bexar County morgue, I visited with Dr. Vincent DiMaio, the head of the coroner's office. As my assigned photographer and I walked into the front of the place, Dr. DiMaio asked us if we had any problem looking at dead bodies. "No," I blurted out before my photographer could answer.

With that the good doctor opened a door, and we were instantly greeted by three simultaneous autopsies. One man was having his head sawed open, another was having his innards removed, and a third corpse was having all of his guts stuffed back into his open body cavity which made a greasy squeaking sound and caused the dead man's limbs to jump up and down as if he were being applied electric shock. The idea, of course, was to shock us and Dr. DiMaio was effective on that score. Later on, an interview inside the morgue's cooler sparked another round of shock. As we sat quietly discussing the gentle art of autopsies and crime solving we all began to hear a soft moaning sound from inside the cooler.

My photographer looked at me and I at him. Then I looked at the doctor. "I know I didn't make that sound," I said. "And I know my photographer didn't, and I was looking at you so I'm pretty sure you didn't, so who did?"

I looked around the cooler and there were only three other people in there with us and none of them were alive. At least I was reasonably sure of that as all three of the bodies had the big "Y" incision cut in them from pubis to neck and all of them were very, very pale, and not a one of them moved during the entire time we were in the cooler.

"It's gas," the doctor said.

"I've never passed gas that sounded like that doc," my photographer volunteered. "You might need help."

But the doctor wasn't talking about us. As he explained it, gas escaping from a dead body will sometimes pass over the vocal chords creating a very spooky moaning sound from a dead body.

Wonderful. Equally wonderful was what happened when a corpse that had experienced arthritis in life was not strapped into his metal gurney in death. The said corpse has a tendency, once rigor mortis sets in, to constrict. Which means a corpse lying flat on its back will sometimes rise up into a sitting position. As Dr. DiMaio explained it, such an occurrence once caused an attendant to flee in terror.

"Can you imagine," The doctor said, stifling a laugh.

No. That sort of thing happens to me every day.

Keeping a sense of humor while covering crime quickly becomes everyone's best defense against going nuts with everything you're apt to see in a criminal setting. One night, while spending a weekend in the Alazon Apache courts for a series on crime in the barrio I found myself waking to the sound of gun fire- apparently the universal form of greeting among drunken teenagers in the 'hood.

Realizing that we had a potential story, my photographer, Tony Ruiz, and I gathered our wits and our equipment and headed out the door. Directly behind the small apartment we were sharing with a family of four, we found a young man of about 19 and his older uncle sitting on the porch of another small apartment. The older man was screaming in pain while his nephew waved a .357 Magnum around.

"I told you not to drink that beer," the young man said.

The old man was too drunk and hurt to do anything but scream obscenities in Spanish at his nephew. "Cabrone, Chingado," he shouted loudly and often.

We rolled up and didn't expect to see a shooting still ongoing, so naturally we were a little reticent to enter the scene. Then the nephew saw us, and I expected the worst. But we didn't get shot at. Instead the nephew began waving around his gun.

"Hey, Channel 4. Channel 4," the kid shouted. "I'm going to be on television. I told my uncle not to drink the last cerveza."

I was right. I expected the worst, and I got it.

But the kid seemed as happy as a bride ready to marry a multimillionaire on Fox television. His joy lasted about as long, too, for soon the ambulance and a cop came rolling up on the scene. The cops drew down on the kid who quickly tossed his gun, realizing his life expectancy was just short of 30 seconds if he didn't.

Meanwhile the uncle continued to scream in pain as the paramedics tried to work with him.

"My knee! My knee!" The uncle shouted as he clutched at his bloody leg.

"I know," said the paramedic. "I've got it right here in my hand," he added as he displayed the man's knee cap to him.

Apparently paramedics need a sense of humor too.

Street cops have developed a keen sense of gallows humor as well.

Spin Control

Some of the smartest, and by that I mean those with the most common sense, were the beat cops I met and knew in San Antonio. Far removed from the politics played by the brass there was the street cop who knew what was going on better than anyone in the chief's office. Most of these men were calm and unlike their brethren in other cities, most of them were not engaged in the art of "tuning up" suspects. Their level heads also kept them alive as during the latter 80s their numbers were very small for such a major city.

One night while loading up equipment to ride with a cop on the city's predominantly black eastside (San Antonio is very segregated among its poorer population. The eastside is black, the westside is Hispanic, and the southside is filled with white rednecks. Only the northside is heavily integrated, being reserved for anyone who had a decent income) we heard a gun shot. The cop we were with at the time smiled and took his time. "No hurry," he explained. "He'll still be bleeding when we get there."

Nonetheless, we hurriedly loaded our equipment and drove to the direction of the eastside project that sat less than 200 yards from the eastside police precinct. Upon arriving we found a young man who was the victim of a drive-by shooting. In San Antonio drive-by shootings were actually the preferred pastime- what with footballs, basketballs, baseballs, and other athletic equipment costing so much. After all, any fool with a paper route could purchase a cheap handgun.

The shooting itself wasn't unfamiliar. But what happened next gave me pause. The cop recognized the victim – a gang member. "He's been shot a bunch of times and lived. He'll live again," the cop said.

I looked and sure enough the victim seemed hurt but not fatally so. His numerous bullet wound scars stood as mute testament to previous encounters with the business end of someone's gun. "He just ain't been shot right," the cop explained. "The worst place to be when some of these nuts get in a firefight is to be the innocent woman walking home with her groceries across the street. You almost always get killed then. These guys can't shoot straight."

True to form, a few days later a couple of cops got into a firefight with some heavily armed teenagers on the city's westside. The two cops were armed with six-shots apiece in their .357 Magnum service revolvers. The group of teenagers, numbering four to six, were armed with at least 60 rounds of ammunition in their semi-automatic weapons. The kids opened fire first and managed to hit one officer in an indiscreet location which later gave rise to his nickname "Iron Balls." Other than that the kids hit nothing, although they did their best to empty their weapons of ammunition. The cops, on the other hand, dropped all of the kids and still had ammunition left in their revolvers.

Which is not to say that most cops I've known have all been intent on firing 41 rounds of ammunition at unsuspecting and innocent minorities. Quite the opposite. Most I've known have gone out of their way to avoid using their guns and instead use their native intelligence and sense of humor to get them out of jams. Harold Schott was among the finest officers I ever knew in San Antonio. His beat was the eastside, and he often served as a great source of information on my stories. He knew everyone on his beat and knew what they were all up to. More than that, the people on the eastside trusted him and confided in him. One day we were standing in front of the 401 Ice House, a small convenience store in a shopping center that Harold called the "Shopping Center that Crack Built" as it was reputed that a local crack dealer had erected the shopping center using funds gained from selling drugs. On this particular afternoon we were discussing a couple of stories I was pursuing when a man walked out of the 401 Icehouse and motioning to Harold told him in sign language that a man on the inside had a gun.

We had heard some loud voices in the Ice House as we spoke, but didn't think anything of it. But, we all took it seriously when the man began signaling to Harold about a gun. My photographer, Roy Pedroza, grabbed his camera and we both walked with Harold toward the Ice House. Harold drew his gun. Then, just as we thought the shit was about to hit the fan, we heard Harold.

"Bobby, put down that goddamn gun," Harold said.

"But, Mr. Harold," the teenager said from inside the Ice House. "Kelvin tryin' to rip me off on this soda. He owe me a quarter change."

Harold just laughed. "You want me to kill you for a quarter? Put the gun down."

Crisis averted. Situation normal.

The inherent common sense of most cops is in direct contrast to the stupid duties they are supposed to fulfill. Now, instead of cops, or in addition to being cops, we also want cops to be guidance counselors and to run interventions on families in crisis. I saw that happen once when a teenage boy called the cops claiming his father was verbally abusing him and he wanted his father arrested. Upon arriving at the home, the first thing I noticed was that a crowd that had gathered in front of the home because of the verbal antics immediately broke up when the people milling about saw the television camera.

"That's great crowd control," the cop I was riding with said. "I wish I always had one of those things." Over the years it has never ceased to amaze me how people willing to shoot at each other with loaded guns will run like frightened squirrels when they see a television camera.

At any rate, once we got to the house, the teenage boy came out and confessed he'd stolen his father's car and wrecked it. The father had gone through the roof threatening to take away the boy's telephone, pager, Nintendo, television set, and apparently all connection to the outside world for a length of up to one month. The father hadn't actually hit the boy, although he had threatened to do so. But the child called the police and said he had been told in school of all places that he didn't have to put up with such treatment, and that, in fact, any time a parent threatened a child it was a form of child abuse.

The ugly face of political correctness had reared its twisted head, and, by the book, the cop was apparently supposed to do something like arrest the father or call a family crisis intervention unit who apparently roam the neighborhoods looking for parents who punish their children. Armed with butterfly nets and new-age rhetoric these strange vigilantes are rumored to turn even the most Mastodon of men into blubbering cream puffs of political correctness, but the cop I was with was having none of that.

"You say you stole your father's car and wrecked it?" He asked the teenage boy. "Yes, and he yelled at me."

"You're lucky you're not my son. I'd've kicked your fuckin' skull in. Now go inside and mind your parents."

I loved that cop.

Of course, you could take such actions to extreme. Once while riding with the San Antonio gang unit we rolled up on a house where it was reputed a gang party was going on full swing inside. As we pulled up one of the cops I was with frowned.

"I know this house. The guy who lives here is a security guard for the railroad."

It was a nice middle-class neighborhood and a nice suburban home. It seemed unthinkable to me then that hardened gang-bangers were inside, but the cop I was with remained convinced there indeed were, and he was also adamant about calling the man who owned the house. It seemed that no sooner had he hung up his cell phone than a big, red Ford pickup truck pulled up to the residence. Out stepped a tall, lean Texan who stood at least six-foot-three and was wearing a cowboy hat that seemed to add another foot of height to his imposing frame. The man tugged at his bushy mustache and looked to where I was sitting with the cop in a tinted van across the street from his home. Then the man waved and walked inside.

"Hey, if there's gang kids in there they're probably packing guns," I said. "Isn't it dangerous to let that guy go in there alone?"

"Let's just wait a second," the cop grinned.

A minute passed, and suddenly the loud music that had been playing inside the house stopped. Seconds later the front door to the house opened and the tall Texan appeared with a teenager in tow. The big Texan had the kid at the collar and at the belt loops on the waist of the kid's jeans. The Texan unceremoniously pitched the kid out the front door. He was followed by a second teen who flew about six feet before landing on the front lawn. Soon there were a dozen kids, and a few handguns that had spilled out of their pockets, accumulated on the lawn.

"Jesus, shouldn't we help this guy out?" I asked of my cop friend.

"Shh. Quiet. Just a minute," he said stifling a laugh.

Just then, apparently the Texan's son, also rather tall, appeared on the front lawn. But he wasn't tossed there. He ran out there screaming at his father. Other than the mountain of pimples on his young face he could've been his father's twin.

"You can't do this to me, Dad. These are my friends, damnit," the kid shouted.

From inside the van I said, "This is going to get ugly, we'd better help."

That's when the kid threw a punch at the old man. The punch missed, and the old man grinned.

"Shhh, let's watch this," my cop friend said from inside his van.

"Oh, so you think you're a man now," the man told his son on the front lawn. "Now, we know what you're made out of. Go ahead, take your best shot." The father stuck his jaw out for his son to take a swing at him.

Everything stopped on the lawn. Kids who'd been squirming, trying to get back their guns and assemble their dignity just froze. Everyone looked at the 16-year-old kid.

"Okay, damnit," the kid shouted. Then he took the bait and threw a swing at his father.

Very calmly the father stepped back, and the kid hit nothing but air. That was the good news for him. The bad news was his father had positioned himself to step inside the kid and deliver an uppercut to his son's chin as his son finished his own attack.

The young, pimple-faced boy must've gone airborne at least six inches. He landed flat on his back and unconscious on his front lawn.

"Okay, now we'll help," the cop said from inside his van.

There is a time, of course when common sense and sense of humor fails all crime reporters and cops for that matter. It is when there is a crime involving children victims.

Jennifer and Heidi are the two names that I will remember to my grave. There are of course others that I can never forget, although I never knew their names. There was the little baby boy who was boiled to death in a pot of water by his mother who became distraught because the infant wet his diaper. I see that small baby's body in nightmares.

Then there was the small baby girl who was stabbed with a serrated kitchen knife. The mother reported an intruder had entered the home and tried to rob her and her daughter at knife point. It was a horrible story, but it was untrue. The cops later said the woman had actually used her daughter as a human shield when the intruder burst into their home. That was an even more horrible story, but it too later proved to be untrue. The truth was the woman had stabbed her daughter all by herself because the child wouldn't stop crying because of a nasty case of diaper rash.

Then there was the small 18-month-old boy whose name I never knew. He was killed in an automobile accident south of San Antonio when his mother turned across a divided highway in an early morning fog and was broadsided by a pick-up truck. The baby boy, strapped dutifully in his car seat, was rocketed out the back window of his mother's car when the force of the collision snapped the seat belt holding the safety seat in the car. The boy flew some 40 feet through the air and landed on the cold, wet pavement of the highway, dying instantly when his skull was crushed by the force of the impact. When I got to the scene all I could see were the perfect pink little toes of the dead infant sticking out from underneath of the sheet the paramedics had placed over his lifeless little body. I called my wife in tears begging her not to drive with our 18-month-old son that day.

I didn't lose my composure on the air over that story, nor did I about Jennifer, although I wanted too. The little girl, who was about six at the time, was sitting in a neighborhood laundromat with her mother when an unknown assailant came in, dropped some money in a vending machine and then got upset when he lost his money in the machine. He retaliated by beating on the machine and then stabbed the little girl as her mother watched. The killer then fled on foot and the little girl rushed out into the street crying. When she found a friend in her neighborhood she cried for her friend to look at her intestines which were protruding from the wound. Then the little girl collapsed and died. Her family was never the same.

I couldn't keep my sense of humor nor was I able to keep my composure in the Heidi case either. Heidi was a young girl who was abducted during broad daylight from a normally crowded street in rural San Antonio. She had spent the day at a friend's house. Her friend walked her halfway home and then waved good bye to her and Heidi was never seen alive again.

The search went on endlessly for days as her family prayed for her to be found. False sightings were reported all over town as Heidi was reportedly seen strapped in the back of a pickup or tied down in a car. Heidi's family prayed for her to be found alive and safe, and eventually came to pray that she would simply be found so they could bury her. When her remains were found in a field nearly three weeks later I cried as I reported it live on the air. It was the only time in my life I ever lost my composure on the air. But I couldn't help it. My sense of humor had failed me. The story was too close to home literally and emotionally. She had disappeared less than a mile from my home, and having known the parents I could only feel shame as I had to announce to the world that she would never be coming home to her parents again.

Finally, when I covered another story in Texas for *America's Most*

Wanted I found what a lack of a sense of humor and the tragic loss of a child could do to a parent. In Austin a few years back there was a horrible murder at a yogurt shop. Three beautiful teenage girls were killed. A year after their deaths I came to interview the parents. One mother had lost a daughter. Another mother had lost her only two children, both of them daughters. I went first to visit the mother who'd lost both of her children and she gave me a tour of her home. Her daughters' bedrooms were exactly as they had been the day the girls died. Inside each bedroom was a life size poster of each daughter. The mother looked at them and then at me and told me, "They say you have to go on with your life after a tragedy like this. No you don't. No you don't. My girls are still right here with me." She smiled and looked at one of the posters.

Then I went and interviewed the other mother who'd lost her 17-year-old daughter. The second mother told me a year after her daughter's death she could still "smell" her daughter in her home and at times imagined her daughter was still around. Then the woman burst into tears, and screaming into a pillow, began yanking at her own hair.

There is a reason there is a burnout factor among crime reporters, photographers, cops and anyone else who stands for too long near the fire of human tragedy.

There but for the grace of God go I, and there is a fear I may yet follow.

A sense of humor helps.

Okay, Okay, the Real Story Is...

THERE ARE HEINOUS CRIMES. There are crimes of passion. There are crimes of folly. There are bright criminals and stupid criminals. There are crimes of avarice and crimes of greed. There are crimes of vice and hatred. There are even crimes of convenience.

Then there is the crime committed by Tom Capano. His crime contained all of the aforementioned and much, much more. His was a crime so horrifying in its scope and so electrifyingly stupid in its execution that the denizens of the quiet little burg called Wilmington, Delaware, scarcely believed, when the crime first came to light, someone as esteemed as Tom Capano had committed it.

For those who did not follow "O.J. junior," as one of his own attorneys called the case, Tom Capano was a very wealthy son of a construction magnate and politically connected Democrat in Delaware who was the cock of the walk in Wilmington. People knew him, liked him, and admired him. He and his beautiful wife and four beautiful daughters lived in a sumptuous home in Wilmington that formerly housed a Catholic Bishop.

Tommy had it all but wanted more and ended up dating a string of girls during his marriage, manipulating them and using them as he saw fit. No one, apparently, was the wiser. Then along came Anne Marie Fahey. She was a gorgeous Irish lass with an infectious laugh and a zest for life. At first she liked playing around with Tommy, but eventually bored of him, and in a fit of jealous rage, or random boredom (no one really knows for sure why) Tom killed her. Then he used his younger brother and his younger brother's boat to dump Annie in an Igloo cooler and then eventually deposited her at sea. Her final resting place was known as "Mako Alley" after the mako shark and not some cheap auto body shop. When the walls came crashing in on Tommy, he conveniently laid blame everywhere, finally settling on another mistress, described often by reporters as being so unattractive that she resembled "Dick Butkus with tits."

Tommy ultimately fooled no one with his attempts at chicanery and was found guilty and sentenced to die.

But that hardly tells the story of what happened in Wilmington, Delaware, during the trial, a time and a place that exists in my mind like nothing else every could. It was a bizarre place where grown adults dressed up for prom night every January in a gala event that seems both sad and repugnant- although the alcohol can take the edge off a little bit.

It is also a town of unbelievable contradictions. "Wilmington is a place where everybody either knows everybody or is fucking everybody else," I was told upon my first visit. Scary as that was, some of the nicest and friendliest people I've ever met in my life call Wilmington home- although I'm happy to report I didn't sleep with any of them.

The contradictions never manifested themselves better than during the night we all waited for a verdict in the Capano case. It was a miserably cold, icy night in Wilmington. Inside the Logan House bar, a small group of reporters and attorneys were happily consuming libations at a workman like pace. Joe Oteri, the founder of the feast, raconteur, and lawyer of some renown, was holding court with his fellow officer of the court, Jack O'Donnell.

Both men were heartily engaged in breaking down what they saw as the inadequacies of their foes in a current trial being covered by every publication on the planet: the Tom Capano trial. The case was a convoluted and turgid mess that included every vice known to man and a few that were only prevalent in the lower order of mammals, invertebrates, and a few species rumored to be extinct. In the prosecution's damning summation the cooler that was used to dispose of Annie's body, her last resting place, her makeshift coffin, had been dragged out and paraded before the jury by prosecutors Colm Connolly and Ferris Wharton. Oteri and O'Donnell, two of four attorneys Capano had hired for his defense, were wounded and angry by the end of the trial and the night we all gathered at the Logan House. Capano had demanded to testify on his own behalf despite his attorneys' physical and emotional pleadings to the contrary.

During eight days on the stand, Capano had not only sunk his own case, but his attorneys were hoping to get out of town without staining their own careers. His two local attorneys were just hoping to get out with a minor amount of their dignity intact. So, on the night in the Logan House, Oteri and O'Donnell were happy to critique the prosecution's use of the cooler in the trial. Rather than simply pulling it out to show the jury, O'Donnell and Oteri both said, "He'll I'd've gotten *in* the damn thing." Then they laughed and downed some more liquor with the members of the press who'd accompanied them to the bar.

They really were a good group of people, Capano's attorneys, and one had to wonder what sins they'd committed for God to foist such a disgusting man on them. But, they took it in stride. However, the small town of Wilmington, very small minded in some ways, did not take to the attorneys as well as the press. In a town that had divided itself neatly into pro and anti-Capano factions, the Capano attorneys, no matter how nice were clearly the enemy for most of the population. So, when Mark Fahey, emotionally scarred brother of the dead woman, walked into the Logan House that night it looked like there might be trouble.

I surely didn't want any. I like Mark, and I like Oteri and O'Donnell. I went over to talk to Mark and then over to O'Donnell and then back to Mark. Mark decided to talk to Jack, and Jack, a fellow Irishman, found some common ground with Mark, and they tried to make peace. Unfortunately for me, there was one man who saw me and drew the wrong conclusion. He was a former nose tackle for Clemson, I believe, a rather large man with a fist about the size of my head. He took umbrage with my floating across both paths of the aisle and decided I'd best leave the bar. When he invited me outside, after putting his big ham of an arm around me, I went. Then he tried to shove me down some steps and said he didn't like me. Then I noticed that the bar manager and several reporters had come outside to see what was going on.

The bar manager, a small, little high-strung man scolded the bigger fellah who "aw shucked" his way into an apology, and we all went back inside to drink. But everyone was watching everyone else, and the atmosphere in the bar that night was filled with animosity.

Friendly and mean, engaging and yet paranoid, the entire town of Wilmington was a bundle of overwhelming contradictions and jangled raw nerves.

I blame Capano now as I did then for it. After all, who could fathom the bad, extremely bad craziness that infected Wilmington, Delaware? Tom Capano preached that he was a Jesuit, and, of course, he told us there were no stupid Jesuits, and, of course, as a Jesuit he could lie, but he knew the difference between a good lie and a bad lie. Then, in a court of law he proceeded to tell us he did have the capacity to kill in defense of his daughters.

So how bad did the craziness get? The following, in no particular order, is what the poor residents of Wilmington had to contend with. Even as the rest of the country stewed over President Clinton's peccadilloes and the slight staining of an ugly dress on a fat-ass intern, Wilmington had to deal with some really weird shit:

*Tom Capano testified on his own behalf for eight days (including cross-examination) during which time he volunteered that his girlfriend, Debby McIntyre, had inherited a porno collection from her dead father (which she confirmed).

*He said he called up a friend from jail and told him to go and service Debby while he was in the can because Debby "Has an overpowering sex drive."

*He testified that he and the SECOND HIGHEST RANKING law enforcement official in the state engaged in three way sex with Debby (although the officer testified he couldn't get a hard-on.)

*Nearly every day in the trial we heard these three terms referred to: "colitis," "menstrual cycles," and "the runs."

*Tom said he had bloody shorts and the runs, and that's why he had blood remover in his house - not to get rid of Annie's blood after he shot her and had to clean up the mess.

*He said he made love with Annie only during her menstrual cycle -like any good Catholic I guess- and that's why her blood was in his house.

*He testified that was all right to screw around on your wife as long as she didn't know about it - and was preferably asleep. He said he waited until his wife and kids were asleep before he walked over to Debby McIntyre's house and then watched through her living room window as someone else screwed her. Then he went in afterwards and

"Had different style sex" with her.

*Debby testified she was Kay Capano, Tom's wife, best friend and that she was banging Tom while she also helped plan Kay's surprise birthday party.

*Momma Capano, Tom's mom, whomped Kay with her cane the day the guilty verdict came in (Kay had left and subsequently divorced Tom prior to the murder). "Are you happy now?" Momma screamed at Kay.

*Momma screamed outside the courtroom that Debby was a drunken slut and her Tommy was innocent. Her son Joey wheeled her through a crowd of photographers on her wheel chair, using her as a battering ram as she brandished her cane on one afternoon.

*Of the two psychiatrists who testified during the course of the trial, one collected and made wooden hats, one of which he brought with him into court and was subsequently made the butt of jokes by the defense team. He became known in closing arguments as Dr. Wooden Hat.

*The other psychiatrist was a Dr. Ruth look-a-like who said she wanted to take care of Tom, not treat him. She admitted she was enamored of him and lamented the fact that the man had only six "pairs of undies" in prison. The term "undies" drew a sidelong glance from the judge.

*The judge had an excellent sense of humor. During jury voir dire he questioned a potential juror on whether or not he had seen any news coverage of the Capano case. When the juror said yes he had, the judge then asked the juror if he had formed an opinion. The potential juror said yes and then went on to say that he thought Capano "Was guilty as sin and should plead guilty to maybe save his life and save the state of Delaware the cost of having to prosecute your ass." The judge excused the juror and then turned to the defense team. "Would the defense like a moment to consider the man's proposition?" he slyly asked.

*On the day the jury reached a verdict, the prosecution, the judge and the Fahey family were greeted with cheers from the hundreds of people assembled outside the court house. The defense team was heckled by a nut who was shooed away by the press.

*Kay Capano says the day after Annie disappeared Tom came over to her house and on the back deck told her he would be a suspect in the missing person's case. He had borrowed Kay's blue Suburban the day of the disappearance, and Kay immediately put two and two together.

"You bastard, you used my car to dump the body didn't you?"

"That's exactly why we're not married any more Kay," is all that Tom said.

*The day the sentence was handed down by the jury, two guys in dark shades drove around the courthouse square in a '65 cherry red convertible with a horn that blared the theme from *The Godfather*. Hundreds of people were serenaded by that tune. When the defense team came outside to greet the press lead attorney Joe Oteri shouted "asshole" into live television cameras as the theme from *The Godfather* played yet again.

*Tom gave his home phone number and pictures of his girls to a child molester in prison as payoff for testimony against another prisoner. Consequently, according to Kay, prisoners have been calling her house for the last two months offering to get together with her girls after they get out of prison.

*When Jack O'Donnell, one of the defense attorneys, used this as evidence to the girls that their father wasn't the man he used to be he said, "Now would the father you know ever let you talk to a child molester?" Alex, the youngest daughter said, "Hell, no. He wouldn't even let us talk to kids who went to public school."

*Tom started off one of the letters to Debby in prison by saying "I hope this letter finds you on all fours getting a stiff cock in your mouth."

*He called another mistress his "slutty little girl." He then called this mistress back as a character witness during the penalty phase of the trial. "He wanted to smell her puss one more time," his own attorney said.

*He testified that at one time he was dating as many as nine women at once - and that he enjoyed sexual threesomes whenever possible.

*A woman with whom he'd had a casual fling explained that women were attracted to Tom Capano because of his money. She claimed Tom had a little tiny penis that would get hard, but it was a quick ride, and, as a woman, you had to jump on and off rather quickly.

But the bad craziness that was rampant in Delaware did not cease when Capano was sentenced to die and the case slowly faded away. No, Judge William Swain Lee, the man who had presided with such impeccable grace and charm during the trial decided to run for governor. This would put him in the awkward position of being able to grant a reprieve to a man he'd sentenced die, if he so desired and was elected. During the course of the campaign, Lee also divulged to the press that Capano had tried to call one of his daughters as a witness and was encouraging the daughter to perjure herself. That revelation was part of sealed proceedings in the judge's chambers and was cause for a slap on the wrist to the Judge.

Capano fumed and he wrote me on three occasions, once offering me parenting tips, and another time asking me to send him a copy of *Playboy* magazine (with the pictures) because he had little access to masturbation materials in the can.

I left Wilmington divided in my thoughts. I surely enjoyed the friendships I made there, but had to wonder how Capano could've been considered such a great guy considering all that he'd done and all the lives he damaged.

What manner of man can lead such a twisted life? Satan comes to mind, but I think that job's already filled. Too bad. If not, Capano would make a good Beelzebub.

Bozo's Got a Gun

On the last Sunday in April 1997, Rick McLaren and his hearty band of Texas Separatists went ballistic. McLaren, the self-styled ambassador of "The Republic of Texas" was upset. A member of his separatist group had been arrested, and he demanded the local sheriff release the man. When the sheriff did not, two of McLaren's lieutenants marched down the road from their compound and took Joe Rowe and his wife hostage.

Thus began a seven-day standoff with local and state police.

For 10 years McLaren, who once was a member of a militia, had been a thorn in the side of landowners, judges, governors, and anyone else he believed was part of the "de-facto" government.

McLaren filed false liens against land owners, issued warrants for the arrest of federal judges, and asked current Texas Governor George W. Bush to step down. McLaren and his followers believed Texas never legally became a state and, therefore, is, was and shall be forever its own country. But, the state of Texas had other ideas, and a warrant for McLaren's arrest had been issued the previous December. The sheriff of Jeff Davis County, however, didn't serve the warrant since Rick stayed holed up in his small compound with some trusted lieutenants in the Ft. Davis Mountain Resort area. For a while that seemed as good a place as any for McLaren. Everyone knew where he was, and he wasn't coming out and bothering anyone.

Then McLaren started trouble again.

So, rather than raid McLaren's compound, instead the sheriff tried to talk Rick out of his camp, thinking cool heads would prevail.

Then one of Rick's comrades was stopped and arrested.

That prompted the standoff with the Texas Department of Public Safety which ended after a comedy of errors and mishaps seven days later and after being grist for the comedy circuit and the likes of David Letterman and Jay Leno.

THE SO-CALLED SIEGE of Ft. Davis was "officially over." I knew this because, despite the fact that two heavily armed hillbillies in the Republic of Texas (ROT) separatist movement were still holed up in the West Texas mountains, Mike Cox, the Texas Department of Public Safety (DPS) spokesman, came out to a dusty gap on state Road 166 and told me everything was over with- and, after all, police spokesmen never lie.

For three times a day during the past week Cox had come out and told me, along with 200 other reporters, a lot of things. For example, he first told us there were 13 people in the ROT separatist compound. Then he said there were eight, and finally seven. He told us the DPS couldn't keep anyone who owned land near McLaren's "embassy" from entering their property, yet local residents gathered near the DPS roadblock and complained that's exactly what the DPS did to them, and they complained about it loudly. Cox also told us the DPS would share no tactical information with the media, but then he volunteered that the DPS was within 440 yards of the armed compound. Finally, Cox said the DPS never planned any armed incursion into the compound, while other DPS agents told me secretly that not only had the raid on the compound been planned but they were just waiting for the word to go. To say the least, my faith in the local police had begun to waver- that is, until Barry Schlachter, a venerable reporter from the *Ft. Worth Star-Telegram*, told me to relax. "Mike Cox wouldn't lie to us," he said. "He may have committed sins of omission, but he definitely hasn't lied."

To be sure, soon after that, on Derby Day to be exact, Cox emerged from his encampment, sporting a grin the size of Texas, to announce to the sunburned assemblage of photographers, sound men and reporters that four members of the Republic of Texas, including Richard McLaren- had surrendered to the DPS. "We showed the world how to do this thing right," Cox proudly proclaimed.

His statement was undoubtedly meant to bolster Texas and George W. Bush and to put down the Federal government for its actions at a similar siege four years earlier at Waco with David Koresh and his Branch Davidians.

Well, while others nodded their head in agreement, I wasn't so sure what had happened. The DPS had certainly learned a lot from Waco, for all Mike Cox had shown us was a dusty road, two state trooper cars and a half dozen police officers. I was feeling like even though I'd been there to cover the news, I'd somehow missed it. Still, Cox assured me he'd kept us nine miles away from the action for our safety, and I believed him. Really. I mean, I'm no weapons expert, but if we were being told that the ROT had AK-47s that could be fired up and launched over and around hills for a distance of nine miles, then who were we to argue, right?

Actually, I was just worried about my poor DPS friends, especially those in the Texas Rangers. Cox had told us that they had an impenetrable perimeter securing the Republic of Texas compound- which, by the way, was composed of nothing more than a trailer and a shack. Still, somehow the two most violently radical members of the group had managed to escape. That had to be frustrating for the Rangers and the rest of the DPS.

We soon learned that the escapees, Mike Matson and Richard Keyes, III, had slipped from the compound, taking their Beavis and Butthead act into the rugged countryside, where wild javelinas, mountain lions, and starvation might get the duo before the DPS sharpshooters ever could. This bothered me to no end. By now, I realized, this story called for a little bloodletting, and the DPS was in a good mood for it. After all, nobody likes to surround a cabin full of heavily armed nuts for a week without getting a chance to take at least *one* shot at them. Especially the few, the proud, the "one riot, one Ranger" Texas Rangers.

Cox, however, insisted the standoff was over. "It's just a good old man hunt now," he volunteered. "We will get our men."

Well, okay then.

But a few questions remained. For instance, how come the press was still nine miles away? And why were angry residents who'd been kept from their homes near the resort area where McLaren and his rabid band of lunatics had been holed up now forced to get identification cards from the DPS before they could move back into their homes? For that matter, why was there still a "no fly zone" around the perimeter of the area? How could the two heavily armed fugitives escape the DPS perimeter in the first place?

Mike Cox didn't seem to want to answer those questions, and in fact got into a nasty little snit when I even had the temerity to ask them. So despite being thankful for the paycheck to sit out in the beautifully arid hills of West Texas, I became frustrated and bored.

By Monday, May 5th, Cox was nowhere to be found, the heat was beating down on the patch of road where the reporters and camera technicians had camped out with their electronic toys for the last week, and I was sunburned, thirsty and bored. Naturally, I decided to do what I did during the dull stretches in the Persian Gulf War- I struck out on my own in my rental car.

I was reasonably sure I had a better chance of driving around and avoid getting shot in West Texas than I did in Kuwait, but then again it was Texas so as I drove the scenic 166 around from the north I did so cautiously. Passing the McDonald observatory I ran into a DPS roadblock. I approached and slowed the shit-brown rental car to a crawl and then stopped. The tall, lean Texan in his khaki colored uniform and khaki cowboy hat put his hand up and walked toward the car. I could see my sunburned reflection in his Ray-Ban mirrored sunglasses. I looked like hell.

Tex looked grim and determined.

"Sir," he said in his local drawl, "Do you live around here?"

"Was mich nicht umbringt, macht mich starker," I said in my best German accent as I resisted the urge to salute and goose step.

"Sir? Do you speak English sir?"

"Ich liebe dich," I said.

"Sir, do you have your DPS identification?"

"Vass is loss? Papers? I have no papers." I said.

"Sir, without the proper identification I'm afraid I'm going to have to ask you to leave the area," The trooper explained in his best, stilted authoritarian drawl. "There is a police action going on here right now."

I smiled, thought about it for a moment, and again resisting the urge to goose step and salute, I got into the rental car, turned it around and drove it away.

When the story first broke, I was actually looking forward to my trip to West Texas. The last time I'd been in the vicinity of Ft. Davis was during the 1991 unveiling of the Federal Government's big white blimp that was to be used to deter drug smuggling. It's a low-level detection unit that was all set to be attached to a tether line near Marfa, Texas, and Sen. Phil Gramm showed up for its inaugural launch. I had flown into Marfa on a Black Hawk helicopter about 50 feet off the deck. It was quite an experience, a hell of an adrenaline rush and a great way to see the countryside.

I'm told by the way that the drug detection blimp has been replaced at least twice since its inauguration because it's been struck by lightning and burst. But on the upside, say the locals, not one drug smuggler has been caught because of the blimp, and all for a cost of millions of tax dollars. When I called the DEA to confirm this, a spokesperson admitted she did not know if the blimp had been "directly responsible" for any drug smuggling arrests, but said "it has been a valuable tool for law enforcement since its launching, nonetheless."

Well, okay, then.

Ft. Davis, the seat of Jeff Davis County, is a dry, West Texas version of Mayberry. The local Sheriff has just two deputies. There's one doctor in town, and a resident proudly told me they'd just gotten their first lawyer. There's only one liquor store in town and one bar which is a private club. Naturally, once the siege began, the saloon became the social hub for all the journalists who could spare a moment to quench their thirsts. In one case it even served as a perfect place for a television producer to celebrate his 39th birthday.

The small town (pop. 1200) sits just north of Marfa, home the mysterious "Marfa lights," and about four hours south of Roswell, New Mexico, mecca to UFO enthusiasts around the world. This could go a long way to explaining Rick McLaren's odd behavior, except he isn't a native of West Texas, nor Texas at all.

Although the town could be pegged as your typical West Texas redneck outpost, the denizens of Ft. Davis and the nearby communities display an attitude of tolerance and acceptance that rivals the big cities of the Northeast. How else could you explain the fact that no one shot at, nor hanged, Rick McLaren in the last eleven years? God knows everyone in Ft. Davis wanted to, and there are no shortages of guns or rope in the arid high plains of that area. McLaren had filed bogus liens against every landowner in Jeff Davis county and harassed local residents with his peculiar and offbeat brand of patriotism for at least a decade.

When residents gathered for a town meeting with DPS officials on Friday night, May 2nd, the frustration the locals had felt bubbled to the surface. A half dozen DPS spokesmen squirmed as their feet were held to the fire by residents who were pissed at the DPS, pissed at the situation in general and ready to string up McLaren. Some were upset about the DPS forcing them from their homes, when, in many cases, those homes were miles from McLaren's property. Others were upset that livestock weren't getting fed, or that elderly residents, men and women who had simply refused to come out, were stuck inside the police perimeter missing vital medication.

Mostly, after a while, the people of Ft. Davis were plain pissed at Rick McLaren. "Why don't you just go up there and shoot the sonovabitch?" one man asked. The proposal was met with a sturdy round of applause. A local teenager followed up by suggesting that since McLaren no longer thought of himself as a citizen of the United States he'd lost the rights of a citizen. Ergo, he was cannon fodder. The woman standing next to me grinned and said, "Get a rope!" Had this occurred just 30 years ago, the lady assured me, that's exactly what the locals would have done- "before all you media vultures and Gestapo state police got here."

For the first time, I thought, the DPS began to look like the last bastion of liberalism in Texas. Maybe there was something about the proximity to Marfa and Roswell after all.

When I arrived at Satellite City- the nickname reporters gave the assemblage of satellite trucks and news units at the official DPS roadblock - on the third day of the standoff, I had a sudden flash of déjà vu. A dozen satellite trucks, a standoff with a radical group, nearly time for the Kentucky Derby. Yep, it seemed a lot like Waco. Of course, it was nothing like Waco. At Waco we were close enough to the situation to at least see the compound and see what was going on. In addition, at Waco there was no buffer between us and the police. There was a line we couldn't cross, the "media checkpoint," but cops lined the barricade, and I learned a lot just by schmoozing them. At Ft. Davis, the DPS kept a 150-foot buffer zone between us and themselves at the media checkpoint. This was a no-man's land, and if you dared step across this line a dour looking trooper with a shotgun would yell loudly for you to get your ass back behind the line. I took to tap dancing across the line whenever I got bored, just to piss off the troopers.

There also was no way to see any action. The DPS barricaded us along a highway picnic area nine miles away from the action. This served the dual purpose of keeping us far enough away so we had no idea what was going on, and of co-opting the only local party spot for the area's teenagers. A couple of teenage boys and girls said the picnic area was the favorite gathering place in the county because it had park benches; there, I was told, the teens could indulge themselves in liquor and pot under the beautiful dark skies of West Texas while having the added advantage of being able to see cops swarming in for miles on either side.

Well, okay then.

It boiled down to this: In covering a standoff between police and dangerous separatists, the entire world had to find out what was going on by listening to Mike Cox three times a day as he would meander out to the microphone in the desert picnic area and talk for ten minutes. Most of his answers consisted of "I don't know," "I can't tell you," "We are unable to discuss tactical options," "I'll get back to you," and my personal favorite, "We will have no comment on that at this time."

When Cox grew bored of his own theatrics, and had even fewer bits of information for us, he sent Laureen Chernow, a masterful spin doctor whose ability to dodge a question was only matched by her ability to let you *know* she was dodging the question. It was like watching an android. A question would come in and she would visibly flip through her mental Rolodex, searching for the perfect non-responsive dodge. Apparently, she'd graduated with honors from some special class in media spin. The press corps and I made no secret of our dislike for her. When Laureen got tired of the animosity and Cox still didn't want to show up, then they sent in poor old trooper John Barton. John had *no* information whatsoever. He wasn't even a good spin doctor. One day in particular John was sent out to tell the press corps that the situation was "dynamic."

"What does that mean?" I asked.

"It means it's dynamic," he said. I don't think he was trying to be difficult. I don't think he was trying to be a smartass. Frankly, I don't think he had any idea what he meant.

In the beginning, we all tried to deal diplomatically with this mess.

I took Cox aside after the first news conference I attended and begged for greater access. "It's not that I don't trust you, Mike," I said, "but you've already got a bunch of conspiracy theorists gathering here. It's to your advantage to let us see what is going on so you can protect yourself. You're just playing to the people who believe you have something to hide." This wasn't just conjecture on my part. Local residents said they knew for a fact the FBI was inside, and they were sure the Feds were going to stage a raid and kill the members of the compound, just like they did at Waco. On the other hand, to my eye there never seemed to be any doubt that the DPS was running the show. But without solid confirmation from Larry, Moe, and Curly running the press briefings, who really knew?

All I knew is that I quickly had enough of the daily meat circus with pudgy Mike Cox. I soon began asking very direct questions about reporters' access and was rebuffed at every attempt. Finally, Barry Schlachter confronted me after a news conference and told me I was antagonizing the DPS. "We have to deal with Cox, and he's not being very cooperative," he said, "but I can see you're doing nothing but antagonizing him. There's a time for that James Cagney-type of journalism, but now isn't it." I had no idea what the "James Cagney-type" of journalism was, but at that moment I did feel like grinding a grapefruit into Schlachter's face.

As the days ran on, only a handful of reporters, including Jim Cummins from NBC, would ask similar questions about reporter access. "I think this whole clamp-down thing started with the Gulf War," both Cummins and Mike Boetcher said. Bob McNamara from CBS also agreed. As we all shared anecdotes about press sieges, McNamara recalled the time President Lyndon Johnson, another sturdy Texan, asked Dan Rather if Dan was "trying to gut-fuck him." None of us there knew exactly what that meant, but we all agreed that the DPS was currently doing a rather healthy job of gut-fucking us.

The pleas for greater access fell on deaf ears, and after a while I lost my patience and continued hammering Cox for access during the news conferences. He finally agreed to a pool camera situation, whereby a few select reporters and cameras would be allowed as far as the DPS command post. Then those reporters and cameras would come out and share the news and videotape with everyone else.

Larry Weidman of NBC News was one of the lucky few who made

it inside. "I saw some wine vineyards," Larry said, emerging from one of the first press pool parties. "And the DPS trooper told me this was really good country for wine growing. The climate is great, arid, not much cold."

I laughed. Here we were in a tense standoff with armed separatists who are promising to begin a revolution against the "de facto" state government, we've heard rumors that the group has .50 caliber machine gun and a shoulder-fired anti-tank weapon, and the DPS is talking about grapes?

"[The DPS officer] also told me," Weidman confided, "that there were several electric fences back there, and that he'd found that out the hard way."

Okay- so, never mind that the DPS had taken the unprecedented step of releasing a prisoner from the Presidio County jail in exchange for two hostages McLaren was holding; or that the DPS was negotiating with McLaren via a diplomatic pouch; or that tanks had been seen moving into the area. To hell with all that. We now knew that we could enjoy some primo wine country grapes during those down moments, provided, of course, we took care not to fry our asses on the electric fences.

T-shirt vendors showed up on the third day of the standoff, selling a variety of souvenirs that sported both pro- and anti- Republic of Texas propaganda. Next, the local pizza joints got into the act, running large pies out to the press area, charging us $20 a pop for their cuisine. A local resident joked that Rick McLaren should be nominated for citizen of the year for pumping so many tourism dollars into the local economy. That joke did not go over well. By the fourth day of the event our little Satellite City, which some had renamed "The Republic of the Fourth Estate," had grown to be the second largest city in the whole county. Mike Boetcher of NBC set himself up as the "Ambassador from the Republic of Oklahoma." Other reporters followed suit, dubbing themselves Ambassadors from their home states.

We were certainly taking the situation as seriously as it warranted. After all, the DPS had nicknamed Rick McLaren "Bozo" on their radio traffic, and took to taunting him whenever he would broadcast from his little amateur squawk box.

"Missile one, stand down. Missile two, get ready," McLaren had said one night. "Get yourself ready to deploy the napalm."

Another night McLaren had advised his little band of followers to open fire on the DPS. "Pluck em," he ordered. Nothing happened. Cox reported this to the media, adding that the DPS sharpshooters were taking this quite seriously. The DPS officers I spoke with just laughed. They had McLaren in their sights and could have plucked *him* without any trouble.

The most exciting night for broadcasting came when McLaren began shouting "Mayday! Mayday!" and asking for help from any "friendly nation" because he was being invaded. One of the DPS officers, unable to help himself, put on his best Cheech and Chong voice and began broadcasting, "I have nothing but a Chevy and two gallons of gas, but I'm coming to help you! God save the Republic of Texas!"

Apparently, even some of the DPS troopers were taking the situation as seriously as it warranted.

God knows I'm not a brilliant man, but I have noticed situations like the Ft. Davis standoff seem to breed their own unique brands of wannabes and hanger-ons who are brainless and ball-less enough to hitch their wagons to nuts like David Koresh or Rick McLaren.

At Ft. Davis, these wannabes included the "Pecos Seven," a baker's half-dozen of kooks who, not too long before, had been apprehended near Pecos, Texas, with a load of weapons and (apparently) a plan to rendezvous with McLaren in his compound. Several other men and women were picked up at various locations near Ft. Davis, trying to do the same thing. One man was even captured with two pounds of marijuana stashed in among his automatic weapons. Many in the press corps were saddened when this man was arrested. There was hope he would at least make it to Satellite City. Or at least his marijuana would.

Then there was Ron Beames. Ron made national news shoving a DPS trooper on the first day of the standoff, and then quickly took his newfound fame to unseen heights –at least for a man who makes his living renting horses for trail rides in West Texas. Two days after he shoved a cop, Ron was back before the microphones declaring that he'd been asked to negotiate for Rick McLaren's release.

"Who gave you the authorization to do this, Ron?" I asked at the news conference.

"The Lord did, brother. The Good Lord."

I, of course, wasn't looking for divine authorization, but something a little more worldly. "Ding!" I said. "The egg timer's gone off, Ron. Your 15 minutes of fame are up."

But Ron didn't get the message. Instead, he dropped to his knees to pray, and dozens of cameras followed him. Some photographers couldn't line up a decent shot, and one even shouted, "Get up Ron! Get up!" Ron patiently waved the cameraman off, and continued his silent prayer while the decadent cameramen jockeyed for a better shot.

At one point in the siege, I found myself dozing off under a big tree on one of the many volcanic rocks in the area. I was just 20 feet from the press conference area, and by my watch I had a good thirty minutes before the next scheduled spoon-feeding by DPS. Suddenly, I felt something bouncing off my cheek and sunglasses. It was twigs and leaves. I opened my eyes and looked up and there was Ron, crouching on a limb some 25 feet in the air.

"What the hell are you doing, Ron?"

"I'm watching the helicopters, brother. They're circling and they might get us."

"Well, go ahead and let them," I said. "But just get the hell out of the tree. I'm trying to sleep."

Ron was hard to take seriously. For one thing, I could never get past the large pink, cauliflower shaped growth on the side of his nose, a boilish bump that seemed to pulsate as he spoke. The damn thing seemed to have a life of its own, becoming especially engorged whenever Ron preached against the government he was convinced was out to get him. "Here's a quarter," a San Antonio reporter had told him at one point. "Go get a rat to gnaw that thing off your nose."

But, the best fringe player in this whole little melodrama was Joe Rowe, the man who Rick McLaren's people took hostage. Turns out, according to Joe, there would never have been a siege at all if Joe didn't love his dog so much. You see Joe, a member of the local Davis Resort Home Owners Association, had been feuding with Rick and his band of merry men for several years, and on the day the siege began Joe actually saw two of Rick's men coming to take him and his wife hostage. Naturally Joe, being a good Texas landowner, pulled out his own gun and had both men in his sights. He only dropped his gun when he saw that his dog was sitting on the front porch, and Joe reasoned he could only shoot one, but not both of the separatists, before his own dog- or wife- got shot. Joe dropped his gun and became a hostage to save his dog- and his wife.

"I really love that dog," Joe said.

It turns out a big dick and a piece of ass may well have been what diffused the Ft. Davis standoff, much to the chagrin of the cops, who were ready to storm the Bastille as the siege came to an end.

I arrived at this conclusion in two parts- the first coming when Julie Hopkins and Lisa Rutlege, Evelyn McLaren's daughters, showed up to talk their mother out of the compound. Terry O'Rourke, who claimed to be Rick McLaren's lawyer at the time, (despite the fact that Rick had fired him at one point) called and told the ladies that if they wanted to see their mother alive again, they should get to the area immediately. Lisa's husband, Rod, being an accomplished pilot, rented a twin-engine Seneca and flew the family there post-haste from their home in the Ft. Worth area. The group arrived in Marfa and waited around for several hours, desperately trying to get to the command post. The DPS told them to go away. When reporters asked Cox why the DPS didn't come to the airport to get them he flatly responded: "We're not a transportation service."

I guess it was lucky for me the DPS wasn't so compassionate. I showed up on a hunch that afternoon at the tiny Marfa airport, only to see Julie, Lisa, Rod, and Evelyn's brother, J.C. Mason, in the midst of a melodramatic little scene. They were standing outside the tiny airport facility; Julie was on the phone, in tears. The DPS had left them stranded, she said, for five hours. What could she do? Well, I wasn't a Boy Scout for nothing. Along with two other reporters who happened on the scene, I eagerly volunteered to drive the family to the compound- strictly for altruistic reasons you understand. That's where the ladies pleaded for their mother's release before dozens of national television cameras. That one little camera-op turned out to be the key to unlocking McLaren and ending the standoff.

As I was driving Julie to the standoff, some 30 miles from the airport, I began talking with her about her mother. Most of the locals didn't seem to know a thing about Rick McLaren's wife. Many didn't even know he had a wife. Julie volunteered how close she was to her mother, Evelyn, a retired postal worker, and how Evelyn had met McLaren, befriended him and eventually married him in a civil ceremony in the "Republic of Texas."

"He seems to be really in love with my mom," Julie told me emphatically, "and she loves him. He's always been a little eccentric, but he's also always been very sweet to Mom, and I was happy that she was so happy. They both said they found their soul mate in each other." Julie also volunteered that her mother had no idea how to shoot a gun, didn't know much about politics and just wanted to stand by her man. That's when it all clicked. If the girls were as close to their mother as they said- and they could actually talk her out of the compound- then there was no way Rick was staying in the cabin with his running buddies.

Why? I've been married for close to 20 years and I know how that argument ends.

"Honey, I want to go shooting, and looting and killing with my friends," Rick would say.

"You can go out, if you want to," Evelyn would respond, "but I may not be here when you get back."

"I'd love to go out and loot, pillage and kill with you guys," Rick would have to say, "But my wife won't let me."

In the end, it all boiled down to carousing or getting laid. That's a no-brainer. End of argument. End of siege.

Less than 24 hours later, first Evelyn McLaren, and then Rick McLaren, surrendered, effectively ending the Ft. Davis standoff and the Republic of Texas uprising. In a move negotiated by Rick as part of his surrender, the couple shared a single cell in the Presidio County Jail in Marfa.

So much for revolutionaries.

Hours after McLaren turned himself in, a tiny old woman approached the Presidio county Jail with a plate full of whole grain pancakes. "Everyone needs their whole grain goodness," the little woman told a dozen cameras who tripped over themselves looking for something, anything, to put on videotape. The little woman said she was a member of the Republic of Texas, and then she railed against the de facto government, Governor George Bush and the lack of whole grain goodness in everyone's diet. Then she went inside the jail and handed over her pancakes.

"The pancakes are going in. They're going in," some photographer yelled.

The little old lady gave me a grand idea to get that exclusive interview with Rick McLaren I so desperately wanted. I immediately grabbed my breakfast burrito. "I'm taking my burrito into the jail for Rick," I told the cameras. "I think it's a travesty that people aren't entitled to their daily diet of fat and lard-soaked tortillas."

Then I walked in, holding the burrito as if it were a bible presented by a Priest in a wedding ceremony. The jailer saw me and made a face. "I'd like Rick McLaren to have this burrito," I said evenly. The jailer disappeared to talk to the sheriff and consider my request. When he came back he let me know the burrito could go in by itself, but I had to stay outside. I then felt obliged to let him know I was only teasing. He seemed to have a sense of humor about the matter and later he let me in on his own personal speculation as to why Evelyn stayed with Rick- concluding the second part of my theory.

"Man, we had to strip him down when he came in the jail. The fucker's hung like a horse," he said.

Case closed.

I was told by an astronomer at the nearby McDonald observatory that the skies near Ft. Davis are the darkest in the continental United States. On my first night there, an exceptionally clear one, the beauty was hard to escape. The thick, cloudy cluster of the Milky-Way galaxy shone like nothing I've ever seen on the East Coast and Hale-Bopp comet could be seen in all its splendor hanging low over the horizon. From my vantage point the comet looked to dangle right over the mountain where McLaren and his loyal band of followers were taunting the DPS Texas Rangers. I couldn't see the mothership, but I'm sure the DPS would gladly have sent in some purple shrouds and Phenobarbital if McLaren had requested it.

But, McLaren didn't. Instead he brought in attorney Terry O'Rourke, whose public relations shenanigans turned out to be at least as dark as the Ft. Davis skies. I first saw O'Rourke, who had been hired by Rick McLaren over the telephone, at one of his news conferences he'd held on behalf of his client. Marching up to the television cameras slowly and deliberately, he'd speak in carefully measured phrases, pausing occasionally to make eye contact with various reporters. His was beautifully choreographed television. Just before Julie and Lisa had made their impassioned pleas to their mother on television, O'Rourke had huddled with the whole family in full view of the cameras. He seemed to be conscious of the time, permitting them to speak only at the top of the six o'clock hour.

"The six o'clock newscast is the most watched," he told Rod Rutledge, Evelyn's son-in-law. "So, we're going to speak at that time. Then we're going to ask the reporters to allow us to leave."

O'Rourke may be from Texas, but he's got the timing of a Capitol Hill pro. Later that evening, I ran into O'Rourke in the small town of Ft. Davis. I congratulated him on a marvelous manipulation of the camera. He smiled and put his arm around me as if we'd been friends for 20 years. "What do you think I should do next?" he asked.

"Uh, you're the lawyer, surely you have a plan," I said.

"Well, I think I can trot the family out for some more tears at least one more time tomorrow. Those girls are great. The whole world saw they're not white trash. This is a good all-American family," he said.

It's Saturday night, May 3rd, and I still don't know who won the Derby. For a Kentucky boy, a Derby day without a mint julep and a racing form is nothing short of sacrilege. Then again, I did do penance by downing several shots of Jim Beam with a few friends. Eventually, we passed time commiserating over the standoff.

"It's not about journalism anymore," said Gabe Caggiano, the political reporter at that time for Fox's KTBC in Austin. "It's all about status-climbing and doing what you're told. Nobody cares about real journalism."

Gabe should know of what he speaks. He had seven live-shots "crash" during the course of the week because of technical incompetence; and on the previous Sunday, he had given Rick McLaren's telephone number to his assignment editor, in hopes that the editor would line up an exclusive, on-air interview with McLaren once the standoff began. According to Gabe, however, when the editor finally reached McLaren after several attempts, she decided not to conduct an interview with him, nor did she pass him along to a reporter who could. She simply said the station would call him back later- presumably after the standoff was over. After all, McLaren *was* busy at the time.

Gabe strummed on his guitar and we crooned "Dead Flowers" by the Rolling Stones as we headed out to Marfa to see those mysterious lights. It seemed appropriate. "The war's over my friend," he informed me with all the gravity of a man who's accepted a death sentence. "This whole standoff is just a microcosm of what's wrong. The police stonewall us, the lawyers use us, McLaren uses us, the reporters are lazy and don't care, and management doesn't want you making any waves. Nobody cares. It's the theater of the absurd." Then he smiled and adopted his best Strother Martin impersonation. "What he have here is a failure to communicate." He smiled. "Relax, it's only show business."

By that time we were in Marfa. We got out and looked. I didn't see a damn thing. Turns out the mysterious Marfa lights were a disappointment, too.

Ode to G. Gordon

This ode to the Watergate burglar and radio talk show host was performed live during the conclusion of Liddy's fifth anniversary radio show in Washington D.C.

Go to Hell Gordon Liddy! That's what the Liberals say.
And it's no wonder- you get under their skin each and every day.
They say you're a burglar, a gun toting goon, violent and worse . . .
You pick on President Clinton with rhetoric so terse.

The Liberals say you're a hypocrite, a scoundrel, a bully
And your logic is muddled, convoluted and quite wooly.
He's a Neanderthal, a hellish brute and much more,
He's always ogling women with whom he'll never score.

They say you're mean-spirited and no he-man as you claim - alas.
And I've even heard liberals say they wish you'd kiss their big hairy ass.
Your enemies vilify you, curse you and wish you ill.
John Dean, I've heard would like to give you a mysterious little pill.

But they're all Wrong about you Gordon Liddy. They have no idea what's in your soul.
And I confess finding out the truth was a sad tale of woe.
For the Liberals can call you a violence freak, a sex fiend, a cad,
But this isn't the truth no . . . it's so sad.
That a tough guy, a gun aficionado, and a man the liberals call a dink,
Can be a fan of the wimpy rock group Abba . . . that's what really stinks.

Stories

The White Room

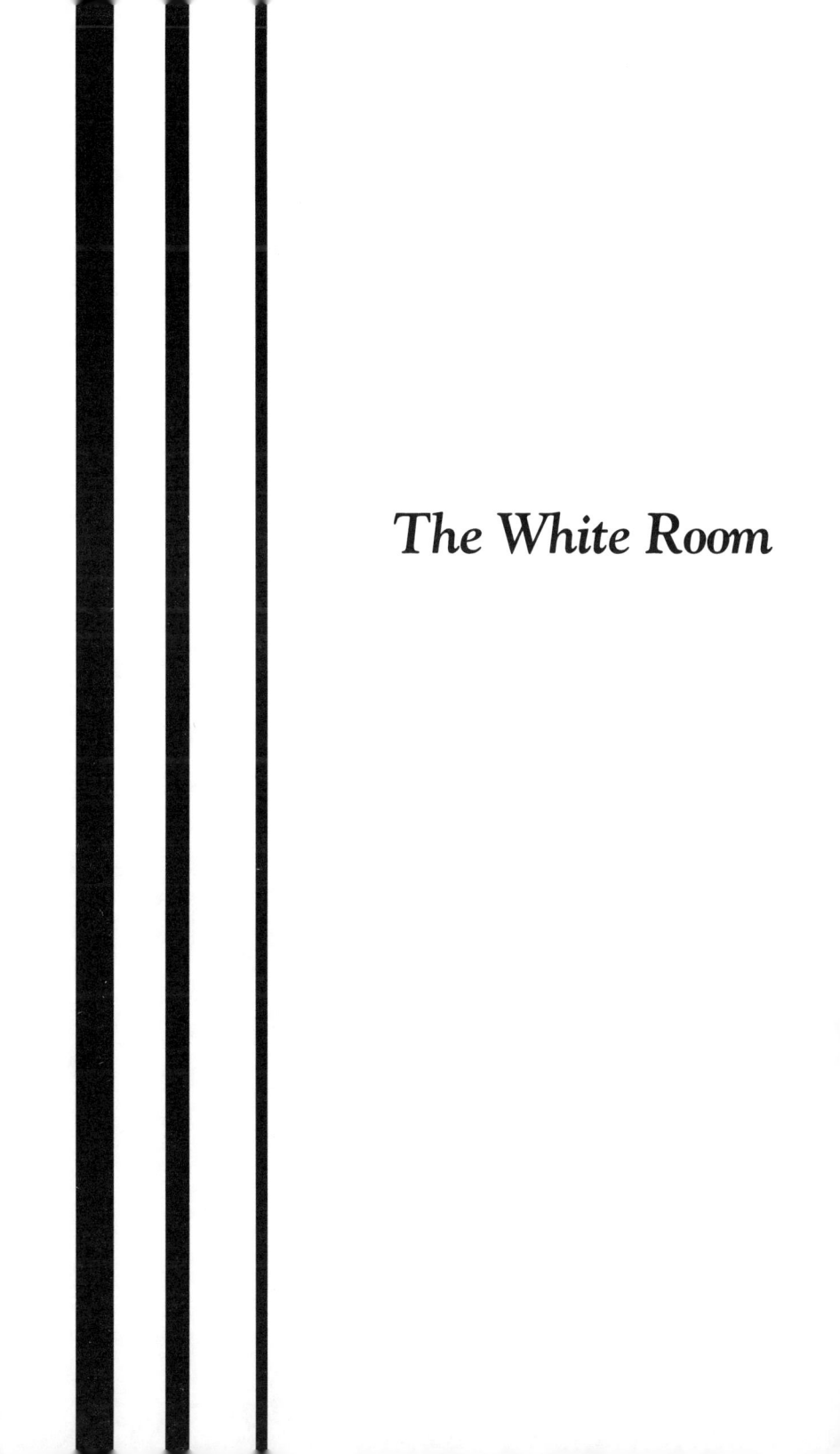

ALL OF THIS TALK of metaphysics and the supermarket tabloid belief that God will appear at the beginning of the new millennium was of course disproved by Melvin Dyatribe in his monumental tome, Divine Flatulence, curiously enough published after the millennium, but apparently no one noticed. Little is known of Melvin's early life before he was dubbed, "The Messiah on Main Street" – a very confusing moniker as he never lived on Main Street. What is known is that Melvin burst onto the national scene like a ferret on Benzadrine preaching the gospel, love, harmony and all you can eat at his restaurants coast to coast for $6.95. Appealing to the masses because of his great Sunday specials – after all who could forget those prime rib slabs – Melvin became the leading Holy Roller at the beginning of the new millennium.

At one time his somber, puffy-fat face graced the covers of Newsweek, Time, and every supermarket tabloid across the country. He was very big in England and especially Wales where he was seen as the third coming of Christ – the second coming having been horribly slaughtered by Welsh authorities when his thick Scottish brogue was mistaken for terroristic threats during a campus panty-raid. At the height of his popularity, Melvin was granted the M.B.E by the British Crown, dined with and was a consultant to three U.S. presidents, and owned his own Hawaiian Island - where he re-instituted slavery briefly to grow cattle for his restaurants before an uprising cost him millions. It was that uprising that changed his life forever. Toward the end, he gravitated to strange eastern religions, worshiping both Broccoli and garden slugs as major deities. On his 55th birthday he officially changed his name to Nigger to atone for his Hawaiian debacle, took up with Courtney Love and formed a new band called Whore. Traveling across the world on an international tour he was renowned for his beautiful hammer dulcimer playing and shocked audiences by pounding his instrument into the stage after every performance.

Tragically, he was to die a few years later while stepping out on Courtney Love whom he'd married in a vegetable patch in Oregon. Courtney caught him in a hotel room with Madonna and Rosie O'Donnell. All four were tragically killed as they shot each other after arguing over Patridge Family trivia. It is highly rumored, but never confirmed that the source of the fatal argument was which child actor made the best "Chris Partridge." Melvin's ashes were co-mingled with Love's and then thrown in the face of Al Sharpton and David Duke during Sharpton's and Duke's nuptials in the Bronx.

After his death, of course, sightings of Melvin continued for years, but the real man seemed to be lost to the ages. Although much of his work, and even his mind, had been downloaded to the Internet where his sexual escapades with Courtney Love sold in the millions for years, still little was known about Melvin's early life. Most especially lost to time was the essay he published that made him such a popular public figure in the first place.

Finally, two years ago a hacker from Hackensack, NJ, found Melvin's first essay buried as an attachment to a file in Steve Case's and Bill Gate's co-authored cyber-book, The Satanic Burses. After two years of fighting with Gate's heirs and Case's mother, the original, uncut version of Melvin's original essay can now be presented to the public for the first time this century.

"The White Room"
by Melvin Dyatribe

The white man, dressed in white, sat alone in the white room thinking white thoughts. Holy thoughts about existence and essence-he could only think these white thoughts.

"What is my purpose? Why am I here?" He stroked his black mustache and his black hair and then leaned back into his white chair once again before he belched a mighty white belch. He admired his white coat and the white walls and the white ceiling in the white room.

"There must be some purpose. There must be a reason for my existence other than mere survival. What is the essence of my existence?" he again asked himself. He turned his head and as if in answer to his question he saw a small, white and black beagle sitting in the corner of the white room. The dog was busy licking his testicles.

"What is this?"

"This is a dog cleaning himself," answered the dog in between licks.

"Jesus Christ. You're a talking dog."

"Perhaps I'm a talking GOD!" said the dog, and with that he finished cleaning himself, walked around in a circle a few times and settled down in a cozy ball. He looked up at the horror-stricken man. "Well, I may be God you know. Think about that."

The white man, in his white suit sitting on the white chair suddenly had an unwhite thought. "How did you get in here? Who are you?"

The dog looked up from his coziness and suddenly was munching on a hot dog that hadn't been there a second before. "It's really a simple matter. You pondered the essence of your own existence as many men before you have. I'm here to facilitate your enlightenment in regards to your deep thought."

"But you're a dog," said the man who apparently had accepted speech from a canine, but not yet could fathom the meaning therein- besides he was busy thinking his white thoughts. "You can't be God," the man said.

"And why can't I?" The dog was still quite cozy and now was sucking on a cherry Icee through a soda straw. "I've been seen by others before. Moses, Jesus, John the Baptist, and Harvey the florist downtown. Although Harvey thought I was indigestion. Finkelstein saw me, too. But he was convinced it was because he cut his curls. Never mind."

"No. I mean you can't be God if you're a DOG!"

"Why not? You prefer a burning bush maybe? I know that's what you called your wife."

"Well . . . yeah. Show me a miracle. Show me a sign."

"I'm sorry, like the d.j. said, 'I don't do requests'."

"You know it's pretty trite if you are God to appear to me as a dog." The man was totally confused. He sat down in his white suit and crossed his white legs trying to re-think his white thoughts.

"You know, you should hold your head up. Hold your head high." The dog/God wandered around the white room and finding a suitable location began to piss. A bright yellow spread across the white floor. Where he pissed a giant white mushroom grew, then exploded into a beautiful white mushroom cloud. Then as the man watched the dog, the beagle took on the visage of a space alien, complete with porcelain white skin and large black almond shaped eyes.

"What are you doing?" the man said in horror has tugged at his white clothing and looked around the white room.

"Rock lyrics. Your type always seems to philosophize through the aid of television and rock music. You all don't think much any more."

"I'm overdosing aren't I?"

The alien/dog/ God walked around to a white stereo and turned on a fabulous old song.

"You're going up to the spirit in the sky," the dog who had turned into an alien told the man.

"Cool," the white man said.

"Prepare yourself, you know it's a must . . . you're gonna go to Dyatribe's Ribs! All you can eat, all night, every night for just $6.95"

"Wow," said the man.

"That's right campers. And don't forget every Sunday night we have all you can eat Prime Rib, cut one inch thick, and swelling with fat for the same amazing low price. Children under 10 eat for free, so fill your soul and your belly. Come on down to Dyatribe's Ribs!" The dog/God swelled to 10 stories high and could be seen on the Jumbo-Tron in Time Square.

"Don't forget, for redemption, reconciliation, and the best meal you can eat, come on down to Dyatribe's Ribs! One free edible Bible will be given away with every meal!"

"I have found the meaning of life. Finally," the man, all dressed in white said from his totally white room.

Tight Shoes
*A Short Look at Life in the 1990's
(a comedy)*

EXT. GROCERY STORE- EARLY MONING
A large three-year-old Ford van drives down a suburban four-lane road, stops at a stop light, then makes a left into a shopping center.

INT. FORD VAN- EARLY MORNING
ELISA, a frumpish late 30s, plump housewife is listening to *The Howard Austere Show*.

INT. RADIO STUDIO — EARLY MORNING
Howard Austere sits at a microphone ranting as is his want.

> HOWARD
> Okay, damnit, who can I insult next?

INT. FORD VAN- EARLY MORNING
Elisa shakes her head disapprovingly. She is dressed to the nines in very tacky clothing. She parks her car, reaches down, and turns off the radio while shaking her head.

INT. RADIO STUDIO- EARLY MORNING
The Howard Austere Show is the nation's leading early morning drive time talk radio show. The show takes place inside a cramped radio studio. On the microphone is HOWARD AUSTERE, his sycophantic side kick, SPARROW SHIVERS, and his producer, DORK BLANKHEAD. As the action begins HOWARD is picking his nose

as DORK signals they are back on the air live.

> HOWARD
> Hey, we're back. And coming up next, we'll see if we can insult some priests. I tell you, Sparrow, you know why those priests wear those black robes? It's so they can hide little alter boys underneath them.

> SPARROW
> (Erupting in a horse laugh)
> Oh, Howard, you're just trying to shock people again.

> HOWARD
> Okay, like I care anyway. Mother Theresa is a whore. The phony bitch. I hope she gets a terminal disease. Okay, I see we have a caller on the line. Go ahead caller, you butt plug (Belch).

> YOUNG WHITE MALE CALLER
> Like, Howard, I think the FCC, like, sucks. They don't realize how brilliant you are. You're just pushing the envelope man. You're great.

> HOWARD
> Shut up, you douche bag. Eat me.

> CALLER
> You're the coolest man.

> HOWARD
> Shut up or I'll take a crap on you. Okay, Sparrow, read the latest news

stories that talk about me.

> **SPARROW**
> Well, the *Cincinnati Enquirer* says you're Satan, the *Los Angeles Times* says you've pushed the limits of good taste, and no one else is talking about you. And that's the news.

INT. GROCERY STORE- EARLY MORNING
ELISA walks into the grocery store and seems to know everyone. She walks to the back and picks up a package of white powdered donuts that have a big red sticker on it that says "$.99". She waddles back toward the cashier. As she walks up she sees that some yahoo with at least 45 items is in the 10 item "Express Lane" so she walks to the next lane which is empty. She puts her donuts on the conveyor belt, looks, picks up a stick of chewing gum, and places it on the conveyor belt. As she does all the lights go out in the grocery store. The cashier, a young, very young bubble-head, frowns.

> **ELISA**
> What's wrong?

> **CASHIER**
> I don't know. But the register's down.

> **ELISA**
> Well, shoot.

She fishes in her purse and pulls out two one-dollar bills.

> **ELISA**
> This ought to cover it.

> **CASHIER**
> Sorry, ma'am. I can't take that.

> ELISA
> Why not?

> CASHIER
> Well, I don't know how much this stuff costs.

> ELISA
> Well, honey the donuts are on special for 99 cents, and the gum is a quarter.

> CASHIER
> Well, I don't know that if the computer doesn't scan it.

EXT. GROCERY STORE- EARLY MORNING
Elisa storms out of the grocery store, gets to her van empty handed, gets inside, and slams the door shut.

INT. FORD VAN- EARLY MORNING
ELISA is cursing to herself about missing her donuts. She turns the van over and drives off. To cool her head she turns on the radio. We hear an announcer's voice:

> ANNOUNCER
> And now back to *The Howard Austere Show*!

INT. RADIO STUDIO- EARLY MORNING
Howard is at the mike with his faithful sidekicks.

> HOWARD
> What? No one is talking about me? Okay, all my devoted listeners have to call up and insult Larry King. You know his mother was a nigger. Hey, what other pretentious celebrities can we make fun of to get people talking

about me?

SPARROW
Now, Howard, you know I'm black.

HOWARD
Yes, you are you fine pickaninny.
Come nuzzle my love gun. Show me
that Brillo bush. You big hairy legged,
blubber butt. Mount me.

INT. FORD VAN- EARLY MORNING
ELISA shakes her head in disdain once again and talks to the radio.

ELISA
Howard, you are so sick. I don't know
why I listen to you.

INT. RADIO STUDIO- EARLY MORNING
DORK, Howard's producer, interrupts.

DORK
Excuse me, Howard? Howard, there
is a caller on the line who's upset with
your language.

HOWARD
Let me at 'em. This will be worth an
FCC fine and at least three months
of publicity. Go ahead, caller.

CALLER #2
(With a nasal whine)
I'm professor Bob White, and I teach
English at Harvard.

HOWARD
Right. And I've got a 10 foot long
schwanz (Belch). Bend over.

CALLER#2
Howard, I think that you're base and crude and appeal to the inerudite-

HOWARD
(to Dork)
Who the hell is this nut? I can't understand a word he said. In-yer-ear-all-nite? What kind of sick twisted perverted is this? (Belch)

CALLER#2
(angrily)
-declining moral values and a sideshow barker who appeals to the lowest common denominator. You prove that P.T. Barnum was right-

HOWARD
(cutting off the caller)
Hey, jewboy, I hope you get cancer. Dork, don't ever give me a caller like that again. Sparrow, why don't you bring your honey pot over here and let me do a Winnie the Pooh. Heh, heh.

SPARROW
Howard, you're going to infuriate the FCC again.

HOWARD
Good I need the attention. Screw the FCC. Screw my audience. Admit it, you love it, you bunch of morons. Most of you sit at home and listen to me when you should be out working a job anyway. (Hack, rasp, belch)

DORK
Howard there's a rabbi on the line who says you're going to Hell.

HOWARD
Great. More controversy. Hey rabbi, you asshole, I'm Jewish. (Loud fart)

RABBI
My boy, you have no idea how you wrong God.

HOWARD
Screw you, Rabbi. That ought to be good for some attention, eh, Sparrow?

RABBI
How could such a nice Jewish boy grow up to be so mean spirited?

HOWARD
Hey, Rabbi, I'm just misunderstood. Ask my fans. They love me. (Retch, rasp, belch)

RABBI
You need such help my son. God be with you.

HOWARD
God? Hey, the big guy can lick my crotch. I hope he gets cancer and dies. Hey, Rabbi, you know that scene in *Reservoir Dogs* where that guy cuts the cop's ear off? Hey, come on down here Rabbi, and I'll cut your goddamn tongue out. Hey, Sparrow, why don't you come over here and put those big black beauties on my fine white

stallion. Heh, heh.

> SPARROW
> Howard. Come on. You've gone too far even for you.

> HOWARD
> Hey you can't go too far. The farther I go the more attention I get and the more money I make. Heh, heh, heh. (louder and louder) Heh, heh, HEH. (RETCH, VOMIT, GASP, CHOKE)

> SPARROW
> That's enough, Howard.

> HOWARD
> CHOKE. GASP- (panicked) I'm ... (choke) Having ... (RASP, CHOKE) a ... heart attack!

> SPARROW
> Come on, Howard. That's not funny. We have to go a commercial break.

HOWARD flings himself violently across the control board clutching at his chest.

> HOWARD
> ... ugggh! I just want to be funny ... Ugggh ... watch my movie ... ugggh *Hand Job*! .. AAAGGGGGH!

He flings himself backward in a violent fit and flops down on the ground.

INT. SUBURBAN HOME- AFTERNOON
Tight shot of a television screen as the nightly news is on. We see the

Spin Control

Anchorman DIM LATHER looking somber as he reads the latest story:

> DIM
> And sad news in the world of entertainment tonight, shock jock Howard Austere has died of an apparent heart attack while doing his show this morning. When reached for comment, Austere's long time side kick, Sparrow Shivers, says there is no truth to the rumor Austere staged his death to promote his upcoming movie *Hand Job*.

INT. SUBURBAN HOME — AFTERNOON
TOM MEADOWS, a dim-witted, balding, paunch suburbanite reaches into FRAME and turns off the television set. He shakes his head and walks past his equally dim witted wife. ELISA. He is dressed in bermuda shorts, t-shirt, white socks, and black sneakers. She is wearing a sundress and looks something like the actress Divine.

> TOM
> Yeah. You watch. He'll show up in three weeks after his movie opens. You'll see.

> ELISA
> You know it's a conspiracy, just like the Vincent Foster suicide.

> TOM
> And the Gulf War.

> ELISA
> And aliens. That's what it all boils down to.

                    TOM
        Come on, Elisa. It's not about aliens.
        Don't go getting kooky on me. It's all
        about the Jews trying to rule the
        world. Shit you know they own
        everything. We got proof on Area
        51. The Jews bought out the aliens
        years ago.

                   ELISA
              Sorry. I forgot.

TOM walks up the stairs of his suburan Maryland tri-level home toward the living room.

                   ELISA
        Where are you going honey?

                    TOM
        Me and Bob gotta go talk to the new
        neighbor about his lawn and that dog
        of his.

                   ELISA
        Oh, okay. Be nice honey. Remember
        I baked Rice Krispie squares for them.
        Take them with you.

                    TOM
        Of course. Wanna be neighborly.

EXT. SUBURBAN LAWN — LATE AFTERNOON
JARED JACOBS, a dark haired man in his middle 30s mows his lawn. He has earphones on and is listening to the Allman Brothers *Live at the Ludlow Garage* and is jamming with "Mountain Jam." He is dancing, playing air guitar and stopping his mowing duties whenever the mood strikes him to enjoy the tunes. TOM and BOB come walking up as if they've happened upon space aliens.

>TOM
>Jesus, Bob. I wonder if he's a drug dealer.

>BOB
>Well, he has kids. Never heard of a drug dealer with kids. Not seen one on the news any way.

They walk over to JARED and tap him on the shoulder. He is unaware of his neighbors until TOM taps him on the shoulder. He pulls the headphones down, lets go of the lawn mower so it turns itself off, and confronts TOM and BOB.

>JARED
>Uh, hello. What's up?

>TOM
>Well new neighbor, my wife wanted you to have these Rice Krispie squares.

JARED looks at the plate and then at TOM.

>JARED
>Uh, thanks, but I'm kind of in the middle of something right now.

BOB, a mousey little guy wearing glasses, speaks up.

>BOB
>Uh, yeah, we wanted to talk to you about that.

>JARED
>What?

>TOM
>Your grass . . . you see . . .

BOB
Well, Jared, we had a neighborhood meeting and we wondered if we might get you-

JARED
Excuse me, you had a what?

BOB
A neighborhood meeting.

JARED
A neighborhood meeting about my lawn?

BOB
Well, actually, about the way you cut your lawn. You see most of us in the neighborhood cut it diagonally, and, well, it looks better if we all did, and well, you cut yours . . . you know straight across.

JARED looks with a straight face at TOM and BOB and then at the Rice Krispies. BOB and TOM have a regular Stepford looking smile on their faces. JARED turns back to his lawnmower and gets ready to pull the string and start it again. BOB and TOM look at each other confused. What just happened? TOM shrugs and taps JARED on the shoulder again as JARED tries to start his lawnmower.

TOM
Uh, Jared, buddy, we weren't done.

JARED stops pulling on his lawnmower and turns around to confront the two dweebs again.

BOB
Yeah . . . uh, yeah, we need to talk

about your dog. You know my wife saw him urinating in the middle of the street yesterday. It really upset her.

JARED shakes his head again.

          JARED
You two are acid flashbacks. That's it isn't it? I mean my dealer told me years ago this could happen and I didn't believe him.

          TOM
Excuse me, Jared, I don't know where you come from, you know I know you're probably not used to the way life is around here, but we're just trying to be neighborly.

          JARED
What do you mean, "where you come from?" I come from Missouri.

          BOB
Really? With that name of yours we thought you were an A-rab or something.

JARED does a slow burn, turns, starts his lawnmower, and goes back to mowing his lawn. BOB and TOM stand watching him as he walks off. JARED puts his ear phones back on and is listening to "Mountain Jam" again and now he begins cutting his lawn in circles, curls and willy-nilly. There seems to be no pattern at all. TOM and BOB don't know what to say, finally TOM talks to BOB.

          TOM
The wife says he's a history professor.

Imagine that.

BOB
One of those free thinkers. Probably has a lot of homosexual friends.

TOM
He didn't even take my wife's Rice Krispie squares.

He holds them up and screams to JARED.

TOM
Hey, Jared you want my Rice Krispie squares!!!??

JARED hears the yelling, pulls the earphones from his ears, keeps on mowing his lawn, and pulls his shorts down baring his ass. He points to it, smiles, and then walks off mowing his lawn.

INT. SUBURBAN HOME- LATE AFTERNOON
ELISA, TOM's frumpy housewife is sitting down at the sofa eating Oreo cookies, drinking milk, and watching television. She clicks a station, then another and finally settles on the news again. On the screen again is DIM LATHER.

DIM
Fidel Castro announced today that Cuba will make a limited foray into the world of capitalism by offering guided tours to the Bay of Pigs Invasion sites. Art Rascamisjuevos has the story from Cuba.

Video package comes up with reporters VO.

ART VO
The packaged tour includes a bed

and breakfast, your choice of camouflage gear, and ringside seats at an authentic recreation of the Bay of Pigs Invasion. Castro also announced that coming this October a similar guided tour will open up on the former missile sites that caused the Cuban Missile crisis. Castro's interpreter explains.

> INTERPRETER
> We are looking most forward to that tour. For every visitor to the silo sites we will give away one miniature Russian ICBM. It is handcrafted and melted down from the real missiles and is destined to become a collector's item. We will accept Visa and Mastercard, but not American Express.

ELISA clicks off the television set and sighs.

> ELISA
> (To herself)
> Damn, nobody takes American Express any more.

Just then the front door swings open and in walks TOM, very mad. He storms down the steps carrying the rice krispy squares.

> ELISA
> Honey, what's wrong with you? And why didn't you give those treats to our new neighbor?

TOM walks down the steps, throws the Rice Krispies on the couch, grabs the remote, and sits down.

> TOM
> Because that man showed me his butt!

ELISA gets up, shakes her head and walks away.

> ELISA
> You must have done something.

> TOM
> Where are you going woman?

> ELISA
> Someone's got to get the kids dinner, and after that I have to get a good night's sleep. I have jury duty tomorrow.

TOM sits and stews. Finally he picks up the remote and turns the channel.

> TOM
> I wish I could kill something.

INT. COURT HOUSE- MORNING.
A typical American courtroom. The gallery is packed with reporters. The jury is packed with jurors, including ELISA, and the judge is packed with his lunch sausage. The room is tense. VINNIE, a small-time photographer sits in the witness chair. He is the accused and his defense attorney, U.R. SCREWED, is upset with him taking the stand in his own defense. RICHARD NEEDLEMAN, the prosecutor, stands ready to grill him and behind him are several victims of the photographer's injustice; Dennis Rodman, Alec Baldwin, etc. As the action begins, NEEDLEMAN is on the attack.

> NEEDLEMAN
> So, you admit you were flagrantly taking pictures at this sporting event of Mr. Rodman, do you not Mr. Vinnie?

VINNIE
Yes, but it's my job.

NEEDLEMAN
You also admit, you weren't wearing a cup at this sporting event.

VINNIE
(confused)
But, I don't play-

NEEDLEMAN
Yes or no will suffice.

U.R. SCREWED
(jumping up and very angry)
That's enough. I object.

JUDGE
(bored)
Overruled. Sit down.

NEEDLEMAN
(smiling)
Now, Mr. Vinnie, did you not show up at a public event A PUBLIC EVENT and take pictures of this basketball player despite his insistence you stop?

VINNIE
Well, yes, I was assigned-

NEEDLEMAN
(thundering)
So, you do admit it!

VINNIE
(wimpering)
Come on. He is a celebrity!

NEEDLEMAN
Oh, I suppose that since he's a celebrity he's not entitled to any sort of a private life, is that what you're saying?

NEEDLEMAN looks over at the jury and gives a knowing look.

VINNIE
No!

NEEDLEMAN
And you freely admit you've taken pictures of other celebrities without their expressed, written permission.

VINNIE
Sure. At public events.

NEEDLEMAN
Do you admit that taking these pictures so upset these sensitive and intelligent celebrities that in Mr. Rodman's case he had to kick you in the groin, bursting, BURSTING one of your testicles to keep you from taking his picture. And in Mr. Baldwin's case, he had to punch you in your face with your own camera, thereby breaking your nose and knocking out three of your teeth before you would stop flagrantly taking his picture. ISN'T THAT THE TRUTH?

                    VINNIE
                    (crying)
        Yes. Jesus, I was in the hospital for
        weeks and couldn't feed my family.

Vinnie now sobs uncontrollably.

                  U.R. SCREWED
                  (standing again)
          Come on, your Honor. Objection!

                    JUDGE
                    (bored)
        Sit down, counselor. Overruled.
        You're not going to get any sympathy
        from me. I've had my picture taken,
        too.

                    VINNIE
        But, it's an honest job! I was in pub-
        lic! They're celebrities!

                    JUDGE
        One more outburst, and I'll find you
        in contempt!

                  NEEDLEMAN
        The prosecution rests your honor.

INT. JURY ROOM- MID MORNING.
The members of the jury, including ELISA, sit around talking about
the case. JUROR FOREMAN is a young, politically correct
neo-liberal.

                  JURY FOREMAN
        I think the fact that he didn't wear a
        cup is very relevant.

ELISA
That's right. I mean he has to know what he's getting into when he goes to these public events.

SECOND JUROR
Well, then it's an open and shut case. Let's see what's on television.

He picks up a remote and turns on a television in the Jury Room. We see the AMW logo and hear RON DAVID's VO.

RON DAVID VO
Coming up next on *America's Most Wanted*, John Walsh will personally choke the living shit out of a convicted murderer. But first this important commercial word from Vagisil.

The JURY FOREMAN changes the channel with a remote.

FOREMAN
I hate Vagisil commercials.

EVERYONE nods their head in agreement. Now we see one of those goofy entertainment shows on the air. It is *Excess Hollywood* with SHEILA SMILES and JOE BLAND as the anchors. We hear the ANNOUNCER say:

ANNOUNCER
And now for *Excess Hollywood*, it's Sheila Smiles and Joe Bland.

JOE
In Hollywood today, dozens of motion picture and recording stars gathered for an historic occasion. Their new

recording of "We Are the World" will be sold to help out state militias across the country.

> SHEILA
> (with sad music)
> Meanwhile, sad news today for Courtney Love. Her new recording of Karen Carpenter's "We've Only Just Begun" has not only bombed, but Love's attempt to clean up her image by recording Pat Boone classics was challenged by Boone in court when he filed suit today against Courtney. Boone, who has recorded Heavy Metal versions of Catholic hyms said through a spokesman that no one had the right to ruin his image but him.

At that moment JUROR #4, looking at the television, turns to his other jurors and says:

> JUROR#4
> Hey, shouldn't we be discussing the case?

> JUROR FOREMAN
> Shut up, Albert. This is my favorite show.

There is a chorus of cries in the affirmative as they shout down the juror and turn their attention to the television set where JOE BLAND is announcing the next story.

> JOE BLAND
> But the big news on *Excess Hollywood* today is the remake of *The Odd Couple*!

SHEILA
That's right, Joe. HootieMax studios announced today that Louis Farrakahn and Jessie Helms will star in the remake of Neil Simon's timeless comedy.

JOE
Farrakahn's agent said the minister agreed to the starring role as Felix Unger.

On the television screen we now see a bow-tied black guy talking piously before the camera.

AGENT
The character of Mr. Unger as played by an African American is representative of the highest qualities of the Nation of Islam. He is neat, prim, heterosexual, and wears nice looking bow-ties.

JOE BLAND is now back on camera.

JOE
Farrakahn's agent said the minister agreed to the role after a week's worth of negotiations and only after first refusing a suggested name change for the comedy. A Helms spokesman says there's no truth to the rumor that the aging senator wished to have the movie retitled *That Darn Nigger*.

Both of the anchors smile their plastic smiles and laugh.

> SHEILA
> Gee, isn't it great Joe when the races get along!
>
> JOE
> Yes, it is, Sheila. And *Excess Hollywood* also talked with first time director Tim Waters, the son of famed filmmaker John Waters about his ground breaking first feature film.

We see the director on screen.

> DIRECTOR
> Uh, well, I know there is a big trend in Hollywood to remake old 60's television shows, and since *The Brady Bunch* was already made, I figured I'd do *The Odd Couple*. My next project, by the way, will be a remake of the old sitcom M.A.S.H. I think that would make a great movie.

The members of the jury turn and look at the foreman who turns off the television set with the remote control.

> FOREMAN
> Okay, let's go fry the photographer.

INT. COURT HOUSE HALL- AFTERNOON
ELISA is walking down the hall. There are a barrage of photographers and reporters. Each one is walking up to either a juror, a celebrity or a lawyer with a permission slip. First the celebrity or lawyer signs the permission slip, and then the photographer takes a picture. Finally, a photographer comes up to ELISA, hands her a permission slip and smiles. She signs it, hands it back, and then poses with a smile.

PHOTOGRAPHER
Very nice. So when does your movie come out?

ELISA
Beg pardon?

PHOTOGRAPHER
Don't tell me you don't have a movie coming out? You'd better hurry. Most of the major players in the case have signed with the big agents already. You'll have to hurry or you'll miss your chance.

He walks off, and ELISA sighs to herself.

ELISA
(Quietly)
Gee, my own movie!

She runs down the hall toward a bank of telephone booths.

INT. D.C. HOTEL ROOM- DAY
We are watching a reporter talking as ELISA runs past him. As the camera pulls out, JOHNNY CARSON is sitting on a bed watching the television report about the photographer trial. He turns it off.

JOHNNY
Uh, uh. I can't believe that photographer only got 10 years in jail. May the dung of a thousand jackals clog his pores.

From inside the bathroom of the hotel room we hear another man washing his face and hands. It is PRESIDENT BILL CLINTON. CLINTON walks out and talks to JOHNNY.

CLINTON
Johnny, I want to thank you for taking this important position within our administration. Mistakes were made. But bipartism reform is necessary. I think having you as our spokesman will help bring about trust in our fine government once again. Next to Walter Cronkite, you are America's most trusted man. Everything everyone knows about trust is here in this room with me. There isn't a thing about trust and honor that you don't know. You are the very paragon of trust.

JOHNNY
Wrong again, Mr. Pasty Thighs. I'm only in this for the money. And I brought you a videotape of someone who knows a lot more about trust than either of us.

He pops a videotape into the videoplayer and turns it on. We see the grim visage of G. Gordon Liddy staring straight at the microphone.

LIDDY
You can run but you cannot hide. Oh, yee 49-percent suckers! There has never been a more corrupt presidency, a more morally bankrupt, sex crazed lunatic loose on the prowl in the hallowed halls of power.

The PRESIDENT looks at JOHNNY who shrugs and takes the tape out of the tape player.

> JOHNNY
> Must be the wrong tape.

He smiles sheepishly, takes the tape out of the television, and turns the news back on.

> JOHNNY
> (con't.)
> Maybe there's something good on the news.

We zoom into see a reporter talking about a Ford van. We see an overhead helicopter shot, not unlike the O.J. slow speed chase. The reporters are following ELISA in her Ford Van.

INT. FORD VAN- DAY
It is trashy and dirty inside and there are remnants of previous encounters at fast food restaurants littered about the inside of the van. She looks out and sees all the media following her and gets upset. She looks down and sees a ski mask in the garbage of the van and pulls it over her head.

> ELISA
> Maybe if they don't recognize me I can get something to eat in peace.

EXT. FAST FOOD RESTAURANT- DAY
Still being followed by the MEDIA, ELISA drives up to the microphone of a drive-thru to place an order. She is in her American made Ford van and frustrated that the reporters won't leave her alone and wearing the ski mask for protection. As she pulls up to the microphone the person inside greets her in a very thick foreign accent. Is it Pakistani or Spanish? Who can tell?

> VOICE
> May I to order you?

                    ELISA
Huh?

                    VOICE
Please, to I you help?

                    ELISA
              (Shaking her head)
Okay. Okay. I want a large milkshake,
uh, chocolate, a large double bacon
cheeseburger, a large fry, oh, just make
it the double bacon cheeseburger
combo and Super Size it. With a
Coke, too.

                    VOICE
Anything please to order else?

                    ELISA
No.

                    VOICE
Price to drive around, please, and
thank you.

ELISA curses under her breath, puts the van in gear and drives up to the window. The window opens up and a dark complected man with a big gap in his teeth is smiling at her. He notices the ski-mask and gets scared.

                    MAN
Is that $5.75?

                    ELISA
I don't know. How much is it?

                    MAN
Please, is that $5.75?

> ELISA
> (getting upset)
> I don't know! How much IS IT? Jesus, can't you just SPEAK ENGLISH?

The MAN seems seized with a sudden fear. He looks at her, swallows and hands her a bag of food. He tries to smile and backs slowly away from the window. She doesn't notice, but he presses an alarm button underneath the register.

> MAN
> Me to you not me hurting. For no payment on my body.

> ELISA
> (thoroughly confused)
> What the Hell are you talking about? How much do I owe you?

> MAN
> (very worried)
> Not on me killed. No money me to take. Thank you.

ELISA is looking at the little man as if he's a space alien when she hears a clicking sound. She looks to her right, and she sees she is staring down the barrel of a police officer's service revolver. The COP has a snarl on his face.

> COP
> All right. Out of the car. NOW!

EXT. DRIVE-THRU WINDOW- DAY
ELISA is yanked out of the van violently and thrown up against its side. She is terrified, and we now see four cop cars, lights on, and a massive amount of fire power and cops trained on her. The media, following her for the trial now is out in numbers covering whatever else new has gone on. The COP cuffs her and yanks off her ski mask.

                        COP
          Okay lady, how long you been in a
          Militia?

                        ELISA
          What?

                        COP
          Is this van filled with explosives? You
          got something against people coming
          to this country and trying to make
          something of themselves? You a postal
          worker?

                        ELISA
          What? What? What? I just wanted to
          know how much I owe!

The COP, having cuffed her hands behind her back flips her around so he can face her. He points his finger into her chest and barks at her. That's when one of the news photographers leans in and shouts:

                  NEWS PHOTOGRAPHER
          You know that's one of the jurors from
          the photographer trial officer. She's
          famous.

The COP looks at her again. She manages a weak smile, but he's very grim.

                        COP
          All right, in the car, lady. I know your
          game.

                        ELISA
                     (Now in tears)
          I don't know what you're talking
          about. All those reporters were

> following me, and I didn't want them to, and I was hungry and I couldn't understand what he said! That's all. Is it too much to ask that the guy who takes my order can speak English? Is it? Huh? I'm not a bigot. I just wanted to know how much I owed. THATS ALL!

She wails and sobs and moans.

> COP
> Uh, huh. You wouldn't happen to be shopping a screenplay would you?

ELISA looks scared.

> ELISA
> No. No, well maybe a movie of the week.

The COP grins.

> COP
> Just as I thought. You're worse than Tonya Harding.

He opens up the car door and throws her into the back of the patrol car while the video cameras roll. When he's done, he closes the door and walks to the front of his vehicle. One of the reporters shouts a question at him.

> REPORTER
> Hey, isn't that a little rough officer?

> COP
> Not if I want to be in on the movie rights.

He smiles, gets in his car and drives off with his prisoner.

INT. SUBURBAN HOME- LATE AFTERNOON
TOM, dressed in rubber shorts and waxed in vaseline, is searching in his bedroom closet for something. There are stilletto heels, leather whips, a leather mask, an enema bag, and other kinky sex toys including a double-headed rubber dildo and a giant phallus. Tom is rummaging through all of it looking for something. On the bed there is a large inflatable rubber woman lying in repose.

>TOM
>Goddammit where is it?

He continues his search and can't seem to find whatever he is looking for. Suddenly the telephone rings. Tom slips and slides his way to the cordless and tries to handle it. It squirts out of his hands a few times before he manages to answer it.

>TOM
>Hello. What? . . . Oh my GAWD!
>I'll be right there.

He hangs up.

INT. BRIEFING ROOM- NIGHT
PRESIDENT CLINTON is standing at a podium, impeccably dressed and delivering a speech:

>CLINTON
>And so my fellow Americans, let me say to you, that this is where we must draw the line. This is where we must come together as a nation and bind our wounds. We can no longer afford to tolerate hate crimes of this type. Mistakes have been made, yes. But no more.

At that moment JOHNNY CARSON steps up and cuts off any questions from the Press.

> JOHNNY CARSON
> Uh... uh, thank you, Mr. President. That was, uh, uh, wonderful. No really I mean it. I'm sorry ladies and gentlemen of the press, but the President can't take any of your questions tonight. He, uh, has to help Al Gore go on a rabbit hunt. Uh, that's right, uh, Al Gore is apparently looking for thousands of missing hairs...

There's a silence in the press room. Johnny smiles and looks around.

> JOHNNY CARSON
> Uh, that's, uh, missing hairs... uh, you know Al is a little thin on top.. Uh, hey, uh, tough room. Uh, well in other administration news it looks like the Red Chinese did apparently try to buy Congressional elections. Chinese leaders are now admitting that it's just retaliation for Americans believing Moo Goo Gai Pan is authentic Chinese food.

There is a smattering of applause and then hands shoot up.

> JOHNNY
> Okay, you, the funny looking reporter in the first row.

The REPORTER stands up.

> REPORTER #1
> Will you be continuing the one liners and monologues at news conferences in the future, Mr. Carson?

> JOHNNY
> Uh, yes, uh, yes, I will. Except on Tuesdays that's when the President will have me walking his new dog- Newt Gingrich. And before you ask, yes, it is a bitch.

The reporters all laugh. Another REPORTER stands up

> REPORTER #2
> John F. Kennedy, Al Gore dancing the Macarena, and George W. Bush after applying cocaine to his penis.

> JOHNNY
> Uh, what are three stiffs?

There is general laughter from the audience.

> JOHNNY
> Okay, great. Well, don't forget our guests tonight are Garry Shandling, Joan Embry, and Jon Stewart. We'll be right back after these messages.

He points to the side of the stage. We hear *The Tonight Show* theme, Johnny takes a golf swing, and we go to:

INT. SUBURBAN HOME- NIGHT.
TOM and ELISA are lying in bed watching Johnny Carson. TOM has on a wig and lipstick and is rubbing his neck with a vibrator. ELISA, stunned is sitting in her nightgown nearly catatonic.

ELISA
I'm glad that Johnny's back on T.V.

TOM
Me too honey... and I'm glad you're all right.

ELISA
Well, I think I lost the movie and the reporters made me look stupid... and, oh, Tom can't you stop massaging your neck long enough to hold me?

TOM
Relax honey, we still got those 50 marijuana plants in the basement to help us make ends meet. We'll be fine.

ELISA
I wish you'd just hold me.

TOM
Honey, you know since I started taking that Rogaine my sex drive hasn't been the same.

She sighs and starts to cry softly. He gets up and walks into the next room where he shakes his head, logs on to his computer, and gets into a chat room. He is immediately sent a message from a cyber pal whose handle is CONELNGUS.

TOM
(visibly excited)
"Where were you lover boy? Downloading pictures of young naked girls?" (typing) No. Had something personal to do. But now,

> I'm ready for you. I'm hot and throbbing.

TOM looks around, gets up, and walks to the door and says to ELISA who's still in bed.

> TOM
> (con't.)
> I'll be in soon, honey.

He closes the door and sits down to type again.

> TOM
> (con't., typing)
> I'd like to thrust into you with my silky tongue . . .

INT. SMALL ROOM- LATE NIGHT
A tight shot of a computer screen as Tom's words scroll across. Then we see Con-E start to type in response. We are obviously in Con-E's private computer sanctum.

> CON-E
> (typing)
> I'd love for you to be with me lover.
> My breasts are heaving in anticipation.

The camera slowly pulls back to reveal that CON-E is none other than HOWARD AUSTERE sitting in his underwear and looking slovenly as he types madly. He smiles, and we FADE OUT.

Spin Control
*(Or: It's God Versus
James Carville and Mary Matalin.
Who Do You Think Will Win?)*

GOD WALKED OVER to his small vegetable garden and looked down at his prized tomatoes. The weather was extremely sunny and warm above his garden, as he wanted it, and the tomatoes were coming along fine. One grew from a flower to a plump, ripe fruit as he reached down to grab it. It tasted delicious. Of course, he knew it would. He sighed. Then, looking down in his pristine garden, free of weeds and vermin- as he willed it - he saw a little gray, diamondback rattle snake. It didn't surprise him. Nothing did.

"Okay, Satan, knock it off. That's an old joke."

Suddenly old Scratch appeared before God. "Well, you can't blame a guy for trying. After all, you were looking bored."

"Yes, I was, you fiend. But, I don't know if I was looking for a visit from a neighbor."

"I'm your only neighbor, bud," Satan replied, a bit sardonically. "Besides, what do you mean 'you don't know' if you were looking for a visitor? You know all and see all. At least that's what you tell me."

"Okay. A matter of semantics. I allowed myself not to know. But, you're right. I could use some company."

"What's eating at you, man?" Satan was worried. He'd seen God many different ways over the ages, but not . . . well, perplexed, which was the only label the old devil could think to slap on the look that waxed across God's infinite face. "I've known you, well, ever since I can remember anyway, and I ain't ever seen a look like that on your big-assed face before." The devil was being as honest as the devil could.

"Don't try and cheer me up. I'm thinking," came God's solemn reply.

"Oh, shit, better watch out. Last time you did that didn't you rain rocks on those poor lizards on Earth? Scattered 'em all like bowling

213

pins as I remember. No, wait a minute. Last time you started thinking you flooded the shit out of that little crap-box. Dead guys was everywhere. The place was lousy with so many lost souls. You know it took me damn near 1,000 years to get those fuckers all processed down in Hell. You really ought to let me know ahead of time if you're going to do something like that again. I need time to prepare." The devil was working all the angles even though he knew time meant very little to him or God.

"Oh, you have a wonderful sense of humor," God sighed.

"Me, what about you? Whose idea was it, after all, to cast Edward G. Robinson in the *Ten Commandments*? I mean, who did he represent, the Brooklyn contingent of the Israelites? Please. 'Where's your Moses now, see. Where's your messiah, now?'"

God shuffled over and grew and ate another tomato. "Well Beelzebub, he kind of reminded me of you."

"Please," Satan feigned offense. "He isn't a thing like me. Believe me. I've had lunch with the guy. He's a big fan of yours."

"Well, I thought you were, too."

"ME? Shit, man. I thought *you* were *my* biggest fan."

God afforded himself a chuckle, but stopped before the Universe exploded from the mirth. Somewhere on Earth meteorologists were trying to figure out why there was a sudden rash of Spring weather in the dead of Winter.

"Satan, really, you never do cease to amaze me. And that ain't easy. After all, I made you. I know you better than yourself. You serve me, whether you believe it or not."

"Have it your way, God. I'm tired of fighting over the matter. You threw me out of Heaven. You gave me Hell. Hey, I did with it what I could, but I'm no interior decorator. Personally, I think you can't live without me. How would you know what 'bad' is without me? Let's face it, you made me as close to yourself as possible with my little personality quirks so you could have someone to pal around with. As they say, it's lonely at the top!"

"Satan, you are a simpleton, but not too far off. But, that's not what's bugging me. I'm thinking of pulling the plug on the whole damn experiment."

"What experiment?" Satan was confused. "Hot toaster pastries, fruit roll-ups, $120 sneakers, what?"

"No. The whole experiment. I think I'll just reverse the entire Big-Bang into one Big-Crunch." God walked slowly kicking at the dirt. Somewhere in the Universe two more galaxies were born.

"Why in the name of all that is holy- that would be you- would you want to do that?" Satan was extremely agitated.

"Bored. Not enough leg room in my S.U.V, I don't know," God said earnestly. "All the pizzaz has gone out of it. I think humans are dead-end. They don't ever think much, they're always caught up in some foolish nonsense, and I have more fun with puppies anyway. I'm a dog person, I guess."

"Hmm, I'm a cat person. That would explain a lot," Satan replied. "But, never mind that. Have you lost your mind? No, wait a minute, if you lost your mind, I guess I wouldn't be here. Or would I? Let's go over that 'free will' clause in your creation contract again, if we could. I mean, really, If you lost your mind, who'd know? Then again, maybe you didn't create me. Maybe, just maybe, I created YOU!"

"Oh, shut up for my sake. I'm telling you I'm getting bored with humanity."

"Big deal, one planet, shut it down. I don't care. You got all kinds of other planets. Some haven't even heard of you yet. It might be fun to go mucking around those for a while."

Satan walked over to the garden to pluck a tomato, but nothing grew for him. In fact, one plant wilted under his touch. "Do you mind?" Satan said. God looked over nonchalantly at the Devil and then down at the tomato plant.

"Oh, sorry." God looked at the plant and suddenly a tomato appeared.

"You're not sorry," the Devil replied as he plucked and ate the tomato. "You did that on purpose."

"Well, yes, I did," God smiled.

"And they say I'm the cruel one," the Devil replied.

"Yes they do," God returned.

The two beings walked around the garden for several moments as God thought. Meanwhile, several years passed on earth and the Chicago Cubs won the World Series.

"Hey, look this doesn't have anything to do with the millennium does it?" Satan suddenly asked. "I mean that's pretty trite if it is."

"No," God replied. "Besides while I've been thinking the

millennium has already passed."

"Oh yeah. Damnit, I've spent so much time up here with you, I haven't gotten back down to Earth. Man, they probably miss me down there." The Devil looked really pained. But, as he looked over at the "Old Man" as he liked to call God, but never did to God's face, despite the fact he was neither man nor woman, but both, the Devil could see his maker would miss him more.

"Do you really want to pull the plug on the whole thing?"

God walked slowly over to his porch swing and another 100 years passed on earth. "The Universe, Scratch, the whole Universe. I gave them my own son. Nothing. I gave them Gandhi. Nothing. I gave them Martin Luther King, nothing. They killed all of them. So, I'm thinking of going Old Testament on their less than holy bottoms."

"You really have flipped your immortal wig." Satan was flabbergasted. "You do that and YOU might as well not exist . . . Oh, MY YOU! That's what it is, isn't it? You want to do yourself in!"

God eased his weary feet out of his sandals as he began to rock on the porch swing. He extended his arm and offered a lemonade, which came from thin air, to Satan who eagerly accepted the soothing drink. "Thanks, man. This beats just about everything else you ever created. Well, except sex and Dr. Kevorkian."

"I'm in no mood," God sighed. "Things are just getting dull for me. There's no excitement. Nothing's new. Dash it all, Satan, what's the meaning? I ain't got no kind of feeling inside."

"What's the meaning?" Satan put his hands on his hips. "Don't you know? What do you want from me? I tempt souls, and catch a few- miss on most of them. I've got a monthly cleaning bill that would choke Donald Trump and most of the souls I get to converse with are real degenerates. You wouldn't believe the number of reporters and priests I have in my lot . . . well, yes you would, but what the Hell. I mean, come on God, you can't be asking advice from ME? You sound like you need therapy."

"Maybe I do. Tell me something good. Tell me that you love me."

"What are you, 'Rufus'? Well okay, I love you, man. You 'da man. And, hey, I know a couple of televangelists I'm going to be in touch with- not to mention newspapers. Man, I can see the headline in the *New York Post* now: God Needs Help! Dr. Satan Provides Therapy!"

"Hey, buddy, I'd be pulling the plug on you, too."

"No shit. But, I wonder, would I evaporate with everything else? Hell, maybe I could be God. Maybe when you pull the plug, evil would still exist! Then I'd be in charge. Heh, heh, not a bad proposition. But, look I've been hanging around you for too long. You ain't getting away that easy. After all I'm Satan enough to admit I need you on some weird, pseudo-Freudian level."

Satan looked over at God, but God wasn't laughing. Boy, talk about your tough rooms. Satan looked glum. Usually, he could goad God into a laugh or two, but not today. "Look, I don't know what you want from me here, God. I mean, to me you sound like a whining teenager. 'I'm bored. I got nothing to do. I know everything, I've been everywhere.' I mean, really what the Hell do you want from me?"

God sat morose in all his splendor and then lifted his infinite head to examine the visage which stood mocking him on his own front porch. "You know, Scratch, when I got rid of the dinosaurs you told me I was acting like a little boy . . . "

"Well, you were. You built them up, you played with them for a couple of million years and then when you got tired of them you just wiped 'em out. Thank you, you didn't give them souls so I didn't have to help clean up that mess, but it wasn't much fun to watch, I can tell you that."

"And now," God slowly spoke, "I'm considering ending it all and you tell me I'm acting like a teenager. Well, at least I'm progressing, am I not?"

Satan shook his heads vigorously. "I'm not going to get into that with you. You'll not lead me down that primrose path. If you want to do yourself in, then do it. But, I'm not going to judge you. If you want that done, why don't you get a couple of your earthly creations up here and let them do that for you. Let the subjects judge the maker."

For the first time that millennium, God smiled. It was a broad, deep and lovely grin within which all things were possible. And on earth a new Renaissance was born as the human race made its first strides into deep space, began colonizing other worlds and meeting other intelligent species.

"You've chosen well, Scratch. I knew you would. That is an excellent idea."

"What is?" Satan was taken aback. "Hey, wait a minute, man, I was just kidding. You know me. I'm prone to hyperbole and other exaggerations. You can't honestly expect me to endorse having a couple of human beings come here and decide whether or not you can end your own existence! Jesus, I mean, YOU, well, whatever."

"Look," God said as he stroked the fur of the puppy on his lap that wasn't there a moment before, "This is my decision. Now, let's make it work."

"Spoken like a true C.E.O. So, what, I've got to pick somebody to come up here and judge you?"

"Not somebody. Somebodies. Two. You said a couple."

"Well, hell. I was talking off the top of my heads. I could have said twenty two."

"Yeah, well, you didn't, so pick me two people. Any two people, either alive on earth now, or who've been alive before, or are currently existing elsewhere in some other incarnation. You will bring them here and they will argue each side of this issue."

Now, the devil was very mad. Sparks flew from his fingertips as he hopped about. "What? You expect me to bring two people here and make one of them argue in favor of you ending it all and another will argue against it. This takes the cake, man. This is worse than that acid fiasco at Woodstock, worse than Richard Nixon and Richard Simmons combined. Hell, it's worse than that free love and AIDS crap that I had to put up with for 30 years, not to mention Ross Perot and the entire Bush family."

God was calm as the Devil vented his rage. "Just make it work."

The Devil turned and ground his knuckles into the palm of his hands. He was always getting stuck with the dirty work.

"Well, all right. But, damnit, I'm not picking any lawyers or judges. That's too damn easy. And no reporters. And NO psychiatrists."

"Pick whomever you wish. The job is entirely in your hands."

"Of course it is. You never want to dirty your hands. Why should you? That's why you made me."

"You know, Scratch," God smiled. "You're a pain in the ass."

"Yeah, yeah. Okay I've chosen." Satan allowed himself to smile. "Actually I think I've done pretty good, if I do say so my own damn self."

"The Devil you say," said the Lord Most High. And he meant it. "I know I'll enjoy your decision."

"You've been saying that since you kicked me out of your cozy little apartment. But, this time I think you're right. These two are the best at arguing. They made a lifetime of it- actually three lifetimes- wrote a few best sellers too."

"Excellent choice," said God. "I knew you'd choose them."

"Yeah, yeah." Satan was unimpressed. "You know everything."

Then, in a wink of an eye, or less, before God and Satan, standing on God's front porch were James Carville and Mary Matalin. Mary was dressed in a red flowing dress which revealed her slim, athletic build, and James appeared in white Nike sneakers, blue jeans and a polo shirt.

"Jesus Henry Christ, where the hell are we, Mary?" James was the first to speak, which was not an uncommon occurrence.

"Uh, Hell is definitely one place you are not," answered the Devil.

"Amusing," said God. "You've definitely outdone yourself this time, Scratch, my boy."

"Yeah, yeah, save it for the party afterwards, God." The Evil One wasn't amused.

"You know," said God, "I'd allowed myself to forget about these two actually. Where did you find them?"

"You know damn well where I found them. They're on their third life on earth. Only James is now a woman- actually a prostitute- and Mary is the man- James' husband and a born again preacher. They refuse to progress beyond Earth without each other."

"Yes, of course I know," said God. "But it's fun to hear you say it. Why did you bring them back here in this incarnation?"

"I don't know," the Devil admitted. "I guess they just tickled me this way. Look how cute they both are. Just like a couple of angry porcupines. "

Mary, who at this point hadn't spoken a word was finally able to gather her wits. "I was born in a blue collar family in Chicago and I don't take no shit. So, I want to know what's going on and I mean NOW," she bristled.

"My momma didn't raise no dummies down in Loo-zee-anna," Carville pitched in, "So, honey, I think we'd better sit tight and see what these two have to say, I venture to guess its important."

"Wouldn't you two rather argue about the Gennifer Flowers or the Monica Lewinsky affair?" The devil smiled; he couldn't resist a bit of temptation. After all, he was built for it.

"Gennifa Flowas?" James Carville screwed his cajun face up into a grotesque display that even caused the devil to take a step back. "Gennifa Flowas?"

"Now, you've done it," said Mary.

"Let me ask you somethin'," James said to the Devil. "If you had this fine specimen of a wife to come home to every night, would you waste yo goddamn time talkin' about Gennifa Flowas or that Monica thing? I mean look at my wife . . . Oh, honey, you do have a fine ass."

The Devil and God both laughed as the Rajun Cajun launched into one of his signature diatribes, and somewhere in the cosmos fertile green valleys sprouted into existence.

"I mean, all these people talkin' about Gennifa Flowas when dey really should be talkin' about how we can turn dis country around and get it workin' right again-"

"If only you Clintonistas would do that," Mary broke in. "Tell me one thing Clinton's done in the last two years. What IS his agenda? Nobody knows?"

"Eight million new jobs formed," came Carville. "NAFTA, the first increases, albeit mild, in the test scores for students..."

"Scratch, I'll give it to you," God interrupted. "When you make a good decision, it's one for the record books."

"Thank you kind, sir."

Mary and James stood and looked at each other. They'd been interrupted! Mary was the first to find her voice:

"You are the two rudest people I've ever met. Now my husband asked where the Hell we were, and I want to know too."

"I can assure you again, Hell is where you are not," the Devil smiled. "Actually, Hell doesn't really exist, well, except as an amusement park. We keep it open for the Catholics and Protestants mostly. They feel obliged for some reason to visit it."

God cleared his throat. "Muslims."

The Devil quickly responded. "Oh yes, well and the Muslims. For some reason they feel they must live there before they move on, no matter how good they've been. I don't know, maybe it has something to do with pork. But, I do get a kick out of those Muslims- especially the fanatics."

"What about the Jews?" Carville asked.

"Oh, well they have Miami" the Devil said. "I don't even mess with Miami."

The dawn of light began to shine on Mary's face as she turned and faced God. "You're, you're God."

"Yes, I am," The Lord Most High responded. "Guilty as charged."

"You look like me. Hah. I was right, God is a woman."

"Ah, you nuts Mary Matalin?" James chimed in. "He looks just like me."

"No," Mary pointed to the Devil. "HE looks just like you."

"Well, one of his heads looks like me. He is a handsome devil. Say, man," Carville said looking at the Devil, "How many heads you got?"

"As many as it takes." The devil smiled.

"And why," James continued, "Do you, God, look like me to me and you look like Mary to Mary?"

"I'm infinite," God said.

"Sounds like Spin Control to me," James said. "Okay, the shock's wearing off now, so what the hell, excuse me, heaven do you want us fo'?"

"Actually," corrected the devil, "There is no Heaven, either. No Heaven, no Hell."

Mary looked at James, who looked at Mary and they both sat down in a porch swing that wasn't there a second before.

"Sonofabitch, John Lennon was right," Mary said.

"Yes, he's an amusing lad. I personally like his post-Beatle tunes better than his collaboration with McCartney, however," God smiled again and peace and enlightenment spread across the Universe.

"Ummm." The devil cleared his throat. "Could we get to the point?"

"Yes, definitely," God said. "We've brought you here to do a favor for us."

"What?" Carville exclaimed. "Da moss Hi n' Mye-dee assing us fo' a fava?'"

"What did he say?" the Devil asked.

"Look, he's a little hard to understand," Mary ventured. "When he met my dad he didn't know what to talk about, so he thought he'd talk about football. So he asked about the Bears, meaning the Chicago Bears. You know, men can always talk about sports. But he asked 'How about dem Bass?' And my father looked at me and said, 'what's he talking about I don't fish?' And James looked at me and said, 'what's he talkin' 'bout. I was asking about dem Bass.' It was a regular Abott

221

and Costello routine."

God smiled yet again and the world felt the glow of a perennial peace. "He's funny. I like him. But, Scratch, he was mocking us. He wanted to know what favor they could do for us. So, I'll tell them. It's this: I'm considering on pulling the plug on the Universe. One of you will argue in favor of this proposition, one of you will argue against it."

For the first time in three lifetimes, both Mary Matalin and James Carville found themselves speechless. And on earth, they recorded one of the calmest springs in hundreds of years.

"Well, I'll be damned." James said.

"You may very well be, if you're lucky," the Devil smiled.

"Well, I'm not going to do it," Mary said. "You can send me to Hell or wherever, but this Southside girl isn't going to argue for the end of the Universe."

"Would it make it any easier if I told you this were a holy thing we're asking you to do?" The Devil offered.

"Don't you blaspheme," James said. "My momma will turn ova in her grave."

"Actually, she's the current President of a Planet in the Sigma Delta Chi quadrant," the Devil said.

"Really?" asked James.

"What happened to our daughters?" asked Mary.

"The oldest is your country's first female President," God said.

"We're getting off point here again. Do you two ever stop spinning the conversation?" The Devil was restless. "All right, let me reduce it into terms you two can understand. Jimbo, you believe in an activist government, do you not?"

"James," James Carville said evenly.

"Huh?" replied the Devil.

"Nobody calls me 'Jimbo' but fat Republicans at bad barbecues. You tellin' me you a Republican?"

"We're getting off point again," God reminded them.

"Right," said Scratch. "Sorry. James, you believe in an activist government, right?"

"Of course."

"And, you Mary," the Devil continued. "You believe that the government that governs best, governs least. You believe people should pretty much be left to their own devices, don't you?"

"You obviously know I do." Mary was still uncooperative.

"Okay, the Big Guy there wants you, Mary, to argue in favor of him having the right to leave everyone completely unfettered. And you, James, you have to argue in favor of a more activist God. One who has some responsibility to those he created."

Mary got up from the porch, clearly agitated. "What the hell is this? Tell me, Satan, are you a Democrat? You cannot possibly draw an analogy between a government made of men and GOD! How can you compare the two? God has created an entire universe-"

"Well, actually," interrupted God, "I've created an infinite number of universes. But go ahead, that's just a minor point."

"Whatever," shouted Mary. "I don't care. My point is God apparently already governs best by governing least. He made the Universe, or, excuse me, Universes, but rarely do you see his hand in the day to day affairs. He seems to let it pretty much go as it will. If, as I believe, there is a doctrine of free will, he has left the Universe to its own devices. Not his. He is a good and sound Republican."

"She has a point there, Big Guy," Satan said. "You know you don't like to get involved very much. You spend winters in Hawaii and summers in Maine. Hell, you spent about a thousand years in the Andromeda Galaxy."

"Lovely place that," God said.

"Do they have good bourbon there?" James asked.

"We're spinning again," the Devil warned.

"Well look here, Devil man," James said. "Mary had her say, and now I'll have mine. I mean, I agree with Mary. God created these Universes, and he seems to spend as little time in them as possible. I think that ought to change. If God is a Republican, he needs to switch parties. He has a responsibility to get involved. I'm right and he's wrong. It's that simple. Now, I'm not saying you should dole out welfare to everybody-"

"Now there's a switch. A Democrat against welfare."

James ignored the barb. "But, I am saying you should give people the tools so they can build themselves a better life. Hell, man, get involved a little bit more. Come down and say 'Hi!' and just let people know yo' around. Shit, most people so scared and worried, they don't even know you exist. They scared of everything. You could go a long way to helping these people out if you just showed up and said 'hi'!

Give people some hope."

God sat tight lipped. "You don't think I do that. How can you look at a sunrise, a comet, a sunset, stars in the sky and not think of me?"

"Shit, man, most people are too worried about paying rent to look at no damn sunrise. They po'. They need nourishment. Spiritual nourishment. All them Republicans talkin' about family values and look at Newt Gingrich. Shit, his church had to take up a collection to take care of his own kids-"

"Leave Newt out of this," Mary said. "You Democrats always want to point at Newt and, you don't even understand what he's talking about. Besides he IS NOT representative of the best the GOP has to offer."

God and Satan sat back and looked at each other as Mary and James continued their argument in the silence brought about by the wave of God's mighty hand. The Devil was the first to speak.

"Well, what do you think?"

"I think you're a pretty sly old devil, there Scratch. I started out thinking about ending it all and you've got me thinking about getting more involved in the Universe."

"Well," the devil grinned. "I can't take credit for all of that. You know, those two deserve most of the credit."

"Interesting, aren't they?" God said as they watched James and Mary continue their argument in muted silence. "Sometimes I amaze myself with my creations." He waved his mighty hand again and the couple were gone.

"But, I'll tell you something and you know it's true. They may be my creations, but their ability at spin control is not of my making."

"Hey, you gave me a job to do. Is it my fault I can do it so well." The Devil just smiled.

"More Spin Control?" God smiled yet again.

And the Devil walked off the porch. "You know it is. Now, if you can excuse me I've got to get back to my chess game."

"Who's the sucker this time?" God asked.

"You know who it is."

"Yes, and I find it amusing that he still continues to play you. He never wins."

"Well, Rush Limbaugh is one of my few permanent residents left and he has to have something to do."

Another Reason Not to Eat Spaghetti
In One Act

Spin Control

Scene I, Act I: *We open on a completely blank set. The walls should be in black. There is no light. Then, slowly, a light is raised. It starts as a burnt orange, dim. It becomes a bright yellow and then becomes a bright orange and red as the actors, who are off stage, begin their lines.*

Man One: Are you sure it was the 67th worse thing I ever ate.

Man Two: That's right.

One: I just can't believe it.

Two: What's not to believe? It happened didn't it? It happens to everyone.

One: But, the 67th worse thing I ever ate and didn't know about it. Why not the first? What about the worst thing I ever ate?

Two: Trust me, you're better off not knowing.

The two men enter bathed in the glow of a warm yellow spot light. As they enter the red lights fade away leaving the stage dark and the men illuminated only by the spotlights. The first man is handsome, but not overly so. He is well dressed and tall, but not too tall. He commands the respect of a generic human being- the type who might be a model for a picture frame or a wallet's photo insert. He smiles and his teeth are white. The first man is also very, very disconcerted. The second man, meanwhile is a study in contrasts. He is much more relaxed in attitude and attire than the first man. He wears a pair of Ray Ban wayfarer sunglasses and has the hint of a spare tire around his middle. It's obvious he has no desire nor inclination to work out. He looks like a beach bum in faded jeans and a t-shirt. The lone exception is a pair of brand new, brilliantly white sneakers. The sneakers seem to almost glow. The two men continue their conversation as they enter.

One: But, what I'm trying to say is why didn't the worst thing I ate and didn't know about, why didn't that kill me?

Two: Timing, age, and a lot of other variables figure into it. You just got lucky this time.

One: I don't know if I agree with that assessment.

Two: It's true.

One: I'm still not sure if I'm lucky.

Two: You don't see any fire. There aren't any red horns around, are there?

One: Big deal. I'm still dead. I don't like it. I don't like it a bit.

Two: No one ever does. Shall we get on with it?

One: Now wait just a goddamn second. I'm not going anywhere.

At that moment the lights flash red, there is a sound of thunder. A chair and a table are seen downstage. There is an old man sitting there eating, eagerly shoving mountains of food into his mouth. It's really quite disgusting. He is a well-dressed man in a period costume from mid 20th century. He is a robust, hearty man whose age shows on his weathered face. But the vigor of youth invades his frame as he desires to consume mountainous plates of spaghetti.

One: Hey! What happened?

Two: We're back at the scene of the crime, so to speak. We're going to take a look at your Last Supper.

One: Hey, that's not funny. What are we doing here? I already know what happened . . . Hey, that's me. See, wow. God, look at that. I still look good for my age.

Two: Yes, you did. As a matter of fact you were blessed with aesthetic endowments.

One: Oh, God. I'm eating a rock. Jesus, it looked just like a meatball.

The old man downstage chokes on the rock, turns red, and pitches forward into his plate of spaghetti, turning the table and the remainder of the spaghetti over on top of him as the old man crashes to the ground. As this happens the lights dim on him.

Two: Yes. I admit there was a vague resemblance between the two, but most of us bite our food before swallowing, Mr. Strawmann. I've seen very few people who have your uncanny ability to imitate a Hoover in full suction while eating.

One: So, yeah I like to eat a little. Is that a crime? And what the hell was that rock doing in the spaghetti anyway. If I were alive, I'd sue.

Two: I must admit, you are one of the more feisty atavisms I've seen in a while. And believe me, I should know. I've been at this job for several thousand years.

One: Yeah, and I got a dick so big I don't need a baseball bat. So what else is new?

Two: You certainly seemed determined to have your own way.

One: Damn straight. I don't like this feeling, and I want some explanations.

Two: Okay. I guess I can answer a few questions. But not too many, and we don't have that long. You've got to get going.

One: Where?

Two: Is that one of your questions?

One: Yes, it is.

Two: Well, you have to leave here. You can't stay here for all eternity.

One: Where do I go?

Two: Is that another one of your questions?

One: Yes.

Two: Very well. You leave here and go to your destiny.

One: Which is . . . ?

Two: How should I know? You think I keep records on everyone that passes this way? Really, do try and get a grip on reality.

One: Goddamnit, that's exactly what I'm trying to do, but you won't give me any help.

Two: That's precisely what I am offering you: help. I've helped millions, perhaps billions in my current position.

One: Well, look. Let's get it straight. I'm dead, right?

Two: It would appear so, yes.

One: Well what the hell does that mean? Either I'm dead, or I'm not.

Two: If you say so.

One: I'm not dead?

Two: I didn't say that.

One: Well, what the hell are you saying. I'd like to know.

Two: You really don't get it do you.

One: What?

Two: You've been asking questions, but seek no answers- not really. And the substance of your questions only reflects the shallowness of your soul. Where am I going? Am I dead? That's all you care about. You're wondering if you'll go to Hell when there is no such place. You stand here, today, not in judgment, as so many of you would like to believe. You are here, before us, for an evaluation. And we can only sum you up as a curious atavism.

One: You say that again. What the hell are you talking about?

Two: You pray to ask questions to seek solutions. Will you answer questions to enable yourself to obtain the smallest glimmer of enlightenment?

One: Now, you're talking like one of them goddamn lawyers. Jesus Christ, I can't stand them. I think we ought to go out and shoot every last goddamn one of them.

Two: Obviously my friend, William, would enjoy that rather crude remark, but I'd like to get on with the business at hand, please.

One: You got a friend named William. What is he, a lawyer?

Two: Please . . . *(hearing no comeback)* Now. Take a close look at the scene you see. Doesn't something about it seem strange to you?

One: Yeah, seeing myself there eating when I know I'm really here seems really weird to me. Any other questions, bright boy?

Two: You certainly seem intent on making this difficult.

One: (exasperated) Making what difficult?

Two: Again you seek to ask questions when you should be answering them. Wait. Perhaps a change of scenery will do the trick.

There is another flash of light and thunder. The chair and the table and the old man are gone. Now, instead we see a younger man standing on a raised platform. He is full of energy, poise and confidence. He stands against a background of people and banners. "Vote for Strawmann!" proclaim the waving strip signs. Action continues in pantomime as the dialogue continues.

Two: Does this bring back memories, Mr. Strawmann?

One: (Surprised and subdued) Yes. It does. Quite pleasant ones.

Two: I should imagine. This is the rally that won you your first election to Congress, is it not?

One: I'm sure you already know it is. It got great play on the national news. Made a hero of me.

Two: (with disdain) Yes. (as he says the following, the action is repeated on stage) You were speaking before a crowd of about 800 people. Suddenly a man rushed from the audience, accused you of being a false prophet and struck you in the face. Security guards wrestled with the man, but you said-

One: (Now taking dramatic control center stage and re-enacting in time with the pantomimed action downstage) Leave this man alone, I say! Stand back and give him room. As was taught by the Golden Rule I will turn the other cheek and give this man a chance to strike me again. Would you like to strike me again, brother?

Two: Whereupon the young man unclenched his fists, pronounced you crazy and then was hauled off by the security guards. (*The action downstage freezes*) As I remember he was sentenced to a year in jail, was given a suspended sentence and was out walking the streets about a month later.

One: It seemed only fair. He had suffered enough.

Two: What you mean is that it was only fair because you paid him $50,000 to suffer enough.

One: (with false outrage) Now, see here. That's a dirty vicious lie that my opponent tried to spread to the good people of my district who knew better than to believe him.

Two: You forget your reason for being here? You forget I know the past as if I'd lived it for you. You paid the man and the payoff was handsome for both of you. He spent 30 days in jail, received a profit of $50,000. He invested that money in an appliance store and sold Maytags until the day he died at age 76 when a washer-dryer combo fell from a truck and crushed him. *(The silent action downstage continues)* You, despite sound opposition, went on to win a seat for your party in Congress. You stayed there until the age of 77-

One: Re-elected by the people, remember!

Two: Yes. And, serving on the Arms Control Committee and presiding over the Budget Committee, you personally sabotaged three arms control agreements under the banner of "No Peace Without Strength." You helped destroy social services, made thousands of young women die trying to perform kitchen abortions, and were directly responsible for making religion an integral part of the government.

One: Thank you. You see, I was a good fellow, wasn't I?

Two: Is that what you see here, Mr. Strawmann?

One: Well, what do you see here? I mean, what are you? A tax and spend liberal who's going to judge me on my life? What is this, *A Christmas Carol?* If it is, then bring on the Ghost of the Past, Present, Future, rattle the chains from my dead partner, and let's get this over with. I have things to do.

Two: Such as?

One: How the hell should I know? You told me I had a destiny to fulfill. Well, let's get on with it.

Two: As you wish. But you realize that you cannot leave here until a decision has been reached about your life. However vociferously you wish to protest, nothing will change that.

One: What's to decide? It appears to me that I led a good life.

Two: Aha! Now we make progress.

One: Great. So I'm through, I can go?

Two: Not so fast. What was it you just said about your life?

One: I said I led a good life.

Two: I believe you said that it "appeared" to you that you led a good life.

One: Big deal, six of one, half dozen of the other. Look, if you're gonna make me hang around for awhile, can you at least tell me if I can have sex any more.

Two: It would appear so.

One: What? Appear so?

Two: You really don't know the difference between appearance and reality, do you?

One: On the contrary. According to you, I've mastered the art- that is if you believe I paid off that man who struck me- which I'm not admitting.

Two: Now who's sounding like a lawyer?

One: Touché. I don't like lawyers, but you spend enough time in government and their ways can kind of rub off on you. So what's the point? That I bent the truth a little? That I manipulated events and conspired to have things as I like them? Hell, I'll plead guilty to that and so would most of the human race. So what? That's life. The one thing I've learned is that you have to control events. You're in charge. You run the show. It's your life and there's no excuse if you don't take advantage of everything and manipulate things on your own behalf. All right?

Two: Well . . .

One: Okay. So I'm guilty. Big deal. It's not like I'm going to Hell. You told me there isn't one. So, if there is no Hell, I'll assume there is no Heaven, and so we're sitting here having the dumbest goddamn conversation I've ever been engaged in. worst of all, I'm talking with some bald-headed Beaver Cleaver look alike who won't let me get on with my destiny, whatever it is. Meanwhile, I'm missing out on whatever it is I'm supposed to do, but I don't know what it is because you keep holding me here. Worst of all, I find out I die from eating a fucking rock, and I've got no one to sue.

A cloud of white smoke begins rolling and building on the stage.

Two: Yes. Quite a display of emotion. Okay. Fine. We'll try one other little gem and see if that won't allow us to progress a bit.

The cloud of smoke now begins to dissipate and we are left staring at a black man standing between several white police officers- who are obviously gripping their night sticks in a menacing fashion.

Two: Now take a look below.

One: Wait just a goddamn second. That's not from my life.

Two: I never said it was.

One: Well what the hell is it?

Two: It may be from the past. It may be from the future. It may never have happened, or it may be going on right now as we watch.

One: All right, I give up. I'll watch. What am I supposed to see?

Just then the black man is struck in the back of the leg by a nightstick held by one of the police officers. The black man falls to the ground and several other officers begin kicking him in the ribs, the legs and the stomach. There are some 56 blows to the man in the next 58 seconds.

One: Shit. What a beating. What did that dumb sonovabitch do to earn that?

Two: Does it matter?

The action downstage freezes and fades to black.

One: What, are you nuts? Of course it matters. If the guy's speeding or something, then I'd say that those cops were way out of line. But, if he was a murderer, then he probably deserved it.

Two: I see. Whether I disagree with that statement or not is irrelevant because I didn't ask you to view this scene in order to pass judgment on the beating victim.

One: Well, why in the hell am I watching some big fat nigger get pounded into hamburger?

Two: You just told me that life is what you make it, correct?

One: Yeah. I believe what I actually said is that it's your life and you have to manipulate things on your own behalf.

Two: Do you think the gentleman getting the beatings did so?

One: Obviously not.

Two: Why?

One: Well, even if he was guilty of some terrible crime, and I don't know and I'm assuming you're not going to tell me–

Two: Correct.

One: But, no matter what he did, he was in control of that situation. He brought that beating on himself, and he could have controlled the situation so it worked out better for him.

Two: You really believe that.

One: Of course. That's my life's credo.

Two: Okay, then, let's watch this.

Downstage the lights rise again and now a semi-clad, dirty, crack whore sits amid the squalor of a horrible tenement with a baby in her hand. She prepares a needle, shoots up, then passes out with the wailing, dirty, baby sitting in a pile of its own feces. The lights dim. They rise downstage, right, where two men in German WWII uniforms are briskly tugging at a crying woman with a gold Star of David pinned to her chest. The lights dim. They rise downstage left on a woman bent over a table screaming in agony as she's being raped in the ass by a huge, menacing man dressed in biker regalia. The lights fade, and all goes dark except for our two men in spotlight.

One: Quite a bunch of scenes. What is it, the porno channel?

Two: Quite funny, Mr. Strawmann. I guess you don't get the point.

One: Yeah, yeah. I got it. The baby couldn't help herself, the Jew in Germany couldn't help herself, and the bitch getting ass-fucked by the Hell's Angel dude couldn't help herself. Women. Fuckin' women. Well, that's my point. Of course babies can't help themselves, but, hell, the mother didn't have to be a crack whore. She chose that. The Jew, while brutally murdered in an oven could've left Germany. She didn't have to stay. Fuck her. The broad getting raped? Hey, what did she do to entice a fuckin' biker, and what was she doing being someplace where a biker could get her and rape her?

Two: So, innocent people should imprison themselves, censor themselves because there are bad people around?

One: Don't even get me started. We live in the real world where there are BAD people. I know enough not to walk in Southeast D.C. at night. Hell, I'm not trudging through Harlem after dark. They'll kill my white ass there. I control the situation. You know this liberal do-gooder shit really gets to me. That's what's caused all the goddamn problems of this country. We want to help the huddled masses yearning to breathe free so we make it harder for the legal immigrants in this country than the illegal immigrants to get help and services. You play by the rules and you get screwed. We created a whole generation of people who've come tobelieve they are victims. It's a crock of crap. My father came to this country from Germany and he never asked for a damn thing. Never spoke German in the home and told us that we had to pull ourselves up by the bootstraps and make something of ourselves. But, you see these goddamn Spics all talking Spanish, saying they're victims and that there's no special services for them. Fuck 'em. Let 'em go back to their own fuckin' country and see if they get anything from the government there. Look at the fuckin' niggers. The fucking Civil War was damn near a 100 years ago and I'm supposed to feel guilty for that? Hell, my parents hadn't even been born. My family wasn't even living in this country. Everyone wants a fuckin' handout, and nobody wants to take any responsibility for their own life.

Two: Mr. Strawmann, I see you feel strongly about this, but you've really taken a rather xenophobic method to your madness.

One: Bullshit. You have to admit that there are too many goddamn people so intent on being "politically correct" that all they are killing this country.

Two: I admit nothing, but if I concede that some people go overboard in trying to redress past grievances, what exactly is your point?

One: That there are damn fewer victims than there are lazy bastards intent on destroying the very fabric of the nation. Take, for example, the *Washington Post*, or as I like to call it the *Nigger Gazette* 'cause you can't even get in that piece of shit unless you're black.

Two: You really seem to have a lot of anger against black people.

One: Don't you mean African Americans?

Two: (*smiles*) Of this I am sure. Fine congressman. The test is now over and you may go.

One: (*stunned*) What? Man I was just getting started.

Two: Yes. I know. And I'm getting bored.

One: (*deflated*) Well, hell. Well, you mind telling me where I'm going?

Two: You already know.

One: What the hell kind of answer is that?

Two: The only one I can give.

One: How in the hell can I already know? You show me two scenes from my life and some dumb nigger getting the shit beat out of him, a rape, a gassed Jew, some fuckin' crack whore bitch and I'm supposed to know where I'm going? I don't even know where I am!

Two: Well that's really unimportant. Goodbye.

There is a sound as if a large wind is approaching. The white smoke begins to billow across the stage again. When the smoke clears, Man One has disappeared.

One: (*voice fading*) Wait. Wait, goddamnit! Goddamnit, tell me something!

Two: Well, all right, since you can't remember any way. You're going back to Earth as a King.

One: Thank you. There is a God. I always knew it. Thanks! Goodbye!

The voice fades completely away as the white smoke billows to immense proportions on stage.

Two: (smiles as he slowly walks off stage) Yes. A King . . . Rodney King.

The Wet Spot

SOUND. A HISS. NO, A VOICE. *Sight. No sight. A blur. Pain. Intense pain. Burning, uncontrollable pain. More sound. Noise. White noise. A hum. A loud, deep, rattling hum. Sight. Blurred what? Faces? Speaking? Dizziness. Inertia. Spinning, unending spinning.*

"Hold on, David. Help's coming!"

A voice. Detachment. Acrid smells. Sweat, earth- metal?

"Jesus, we're losing him. Somebody help me! somebody help me!"

More smells. More loud noises. Screaming? Wait a minute. Fire. The smell of fire. No . . . smoke. And something else . . . meat. No, flesh. The smell of human flesh. Burned bodies and tin can trucks. Movement. Pressure underneath. Swimming images. More pain. White pain. Pure, white, hot pain. Stinging, numbing. Sight. A blur. Fear Stabbing pain. Deep.

"Hold on, damn you. Hold on. Hey, sergeant, give me a hand here. The ambulance is pulling up. We've go to get him in the ambulance."

Tone. A high pitched tone. Again. Mary? Beth? Jim? Sandy? The dog's lost. The dog's lost. Gotta find the dog. Mother?

"Jesus Christ. It's his pager. Somebody grab his pager."

Moving. Blurs. Sounds. Metal on metal. Sliding. Bright light. Swimming

243

lights. *Silver and red, white and silver. Dizziness and fatigue. Shadows calling and crying. Dissolving into blackness. Coming back. Gone again. Negatives and positives. Christmas smells in a hospital. Night of a thousand tonsils. Dad smiles. Ice cream and a G.I. Joe. Dad's hairbrush.*

"All right. Head to Methodist, stat!"
"Will he make it?"

Pain . . . *Spankings at dawn. Fear. Stabbing pain. Not guilty.*

"I don't know. Two shots, one in the cheek. The exit wound is by his right ear. It's shattered his jaw, his teeth, took a bit out of his tongue and may cause him to be deaf. But the one that has me worried is in the abdomen. No exit wound. I don't know where the bullet is, if it's fragmented or what. It's trouble."
"Jesus Christ."
"Is he a friend of yours."
"Yes, he's my partner."
"What happened?"
"I don't know. It just happened so fast. We had staked this place out. We got a warrant and came back to kick in the door. There were only two pot dealers inside. We'd handled them three or four times before. Hell, they knew us, you know. We didn't expect anything like that. David goes around to cover the back. I hear two shots. I run to the back and there he is."
"What happened to the dealers?"
"Fuck if I know. They're gone."

Fading . . . fading. Tired. Bored. Restless. Fading . . . fading. Army basic training. Get Saddam! Burned bodies and tin can trucks. Jail and Hell.

"I've been his partner for three years, and he's probably the best goddamn cop on the force. I'm not kidding."
"What's his name?"
"David Crown. David Ridley Crown."
"Not David Crown the writer?"
"Yeah, that's him. Right there. Look at him. Cop. Writer. Arrogant prick. Shot by a teenage piece of shit."

"He's going. Pulse is low."

Pounding, pounding, hollow pounding. Straw pounding. Drugs. Busts. Stupid inept. Not guilty. Shallow and bitter. Alas . . .

"This fucking driver better get us to the fucking hospital soon."
"We're nearly there. Calm down."
"You calm down, sonovabitch. That's my partner, you fuck."

Movement stopped. Metal on metal. Sliding. Rolling. Fading . . . fading. Blurs and hums. Shouts? Pin prick. Pain fading. Numb . . . fading. Lights. Breasts. Children. Nursery The dog and mother are lost?

"Jesus Christ, that bullet hit every major organ in his chest cavity. Nurse. Clamps. More suction. Two more units of blood, now."
"Doctor, his blood pressure is falling."

First summer on a string. Wind. Hurricane. Water. Flooding. Deep. Breast, breasts in the light. Slept on the wet spot . . . Slept on the goddamn wet spot!

"We're losing him, doctor."
"I know."

Fading . . . the light. The streetlights are on. I have to go home. No medicine, no medicine.

"We're losing him."
"I know."

Slept on the goddamn wet spot!

Free Flight

KERI MOVED QUICKLY across the deck without thinking. Thirty seconds until his shift began. He would not be late. He was never late. Never early. He was on time. Always. Like a well-crafted computer, he clicked into his place, knew his place. In fact, in an odd way he enjoyed his place. He liked the feeling that he helped others, that in some small way he made a difference. He also liked that he never once, ever, had to think for himself. Being detached from the decision making process gave him an odd sense of freedom. He snapped out his binoculars and looked across the deck of the expansive ship. His watch had begun.

"Triplett!" Lieutenant David Thaurus shouted as he marched up to Keri

"Yes, sir!" Keri shot back as quickly as possible.

"Anything son?"

"No, sir."

"Okay, then. As you were." Thaurus turned and marched away.

Keri turned his attention outward, searching with the binoculars for anything, and everything. The ship's electronics were supposed to detect anything larger than a grain of sand within its path, but Force regulations said to take nothing for chance. The human element, by those very same regulations, could not be taken for granted. Keri, along with 144 others, was posted in a strategic position as "eyes" for the ship. His station was at the tail end of the massive ship's bridge, a series of clear plastisteel windows overlooking the tail end of the ship. Outside those huge windows the beautiful blue ocean dominated the view. Swirling white clouds broke up the beautiful blue like thin wisps of floating milkweed. It was an illusion of breathtaking beauty, almost like a painted canvas hanging in front of him. Because they were in such a low orbit over Milsapp's planet the illusion was only broken at the very corner of the windows, where if Keri strained himself he could barely make out the comfortable black solitude and detached peace of deep space.

Jay looked at the screen without much enthusiasm. It was another John Wayne movie. This time the Duke was battling aliens on Epsilon Urandi-5. As usual, his spaceship made a great "whooshing" noise as it cut through the vacuum of space- completely irrelevant since there's no atmosphere to carry sound in space. Jay remembered his mother had often complained about that, but he gave it little thought. Instead, as per his training, he sipped at the Joy Juice near his chin and watched the movie. The dialogue was stilted, and the Duke, although pretty heroic, didn't act like any BAT trooper Jay ever worked with or knew. To make matters worse, whoever wrote the screenplay got all the terminology wrong. To begin with, even though Jay and all his comrades were part of the Ballistic Advance Infantry Troops, no one ever called them "BAIT." Not if they wanted to live very long anyway. The common acronym was BAT as in "Bat out of Hell" for the way they ejected by the hundreds out of a CAP Battleship in a coffin-sized capsule- usually shot right into the enemy's atmosphere to carry on a ground campaign.

But, Jay still liked John Wayne movies. He remembered his mom telling him when he was a small boy that John Wayne used to be a real person, but Jay quit believing that about the time he quit believing in the Easter Bunny and Santa Claus. John Wayne was just a computer-generated hero for the ages. He could always be counted on to do the right thing, to stand up for God and Country, get the girl, and save the small children from the ravages of war. No way, Jay told himself, did such an actor ever really exist. He wasn't even sure there were any real actors any more. Most of them were just CG's. Hell, Jay met a programmer once in a bar who told him even the voices were created by computer. It was all a scam. The screenwriting, however, was still done by real people. That he knew for sure. His brother James was a writer. He wrote a couple of small romance comedies that Jay never seemed to enjoy. They seemed so sappy, and the characters seemed to think too much. Way too much freedom of movement and thought.

They would never survive as BATs.

He lost himself in the happy moment remembering his brother and forgot the John Wayne movie on the screen that sat inches in front of his face. Jay loved his BAT suit. A screen in your face, plumbing attached to take care of your necessary bodily excretions, food and liquid and all the legal drugs available to a BAT trooper were available from the tube stuck in the corner of his mouth. He smiled and felt good. Another quiet suck at the Joy Juice at his chin enhanced the feeling. Nothing to worry about. No cares in the world. The time strip on his wrist said it was noon, ship-time. He sighed. No worries. No thoughts, no worries. Follow the manual, and he'd be okay.

Keri snapped to attention.

"What were you thinking about, mister?" Thaurus shouted.

"I was following orders, sir." Maybe the Lieutenant thought he'd been slacking, but there was not much to see right now. Oh, well.

"Explain yourself, Private."

"The private was executing General Order Number 357."

"And that order, Private, is?"

"The private shall act as eyes for the CAPship as we retrieve BAT soldiers stranded in space from an aborted insertion. Sir!"

"And what has the private found?"

"The private has found dick, sir."

"Very good. Carry on private." Thaurus turned on his heel and proceeded to the next post. Keri didn't give him another thought and returned to surveying for stranded BAT troopers.

Jay studied the read-outs on his computer screen. It had been two hours since the AI. There were several times in his past he'd been stranded in space longer, waiting for a CAPship to pick him up, so he wasn't worried. He wouldn't worry anyway with his regular intervals of Joy Juice, but the spare time weighed heavily on him. He began to think.

"Thinking is the enemy of the enlisted man."

"Yes, sir!" He was daydreaming. Back in boot. Not good.

"Boy, you don't call me, 'Sir'. I work for a living!"

"Yes, Senior Drill Instructor!"

Jay suddenly snapped out of it. Daydreaming was no way to stay frosty. Was this is a symptom of overdosing on Joy Juice? It had never happened before. The manual dictated when waiting for pick-up to stay on the Joy Juice, watch movies, participate in hologram sports, virtual sex, and at regular five-minute intervals check the up-link. He checked his up-link. He was still sending a signal. He would be rescued. That wasn't what was bothering him. He had to stop thinking,

What was it Johnny had said? "I think we're fucked. I don't think the General knows what the hell he's doing." That had been right before the disaster. Johnny was now so much shredded, frozen meat floating around Milsapp's planet. Jay was just a small satellite himself around that small blue marble, but at least he was alive. Why had Johnny said that? He'd made hundreds of drops, just like Jay. Oh yeah, he had a cousin on Milsapp. Why were they the enemy again? Didn't matter. BAT troopers don't think. They act.

A proximity klaxon sounded in Jay's suit. His screen showed a small swarm of meteors ahead. It was a jumbled mass of floating debris from a ship explosion as well as bits of mineral and rock. Man, had this fight been a disaster. Three CAPships totally destroyed. Thousands of troopers like him stranded. Off in the distance Jay had identified two members of his team. No atmosphere to interfere with sighting team members. The detail was exquisite even a quarter of a mile away. One of them was dead of a suit breach. Shit happens.

"Alpha Bravo," Jay said into his communicator.

"This is Alpha Bravo. Go."

"This team leader, Papa Charlie. How are you doing son?"

"Doing fine, Papa Charlie. Got the Joy Juice locked and loaded. Porno on the Holo and I'm good to go for re-insertion."

"Roger that Alpha Bravo. Anyone else on the General Freak?"

"Rogers is a deader sir. Holed by a stray blast. Can't raise anyone else. I've seen plenty floating around though. Debris field making it hard to get close though. Thought maybe my radio was dead 'til you chinned me up."

"We're probably the only two left in our platoon. Stay Frosty. Pickup will be here soon." Jay said. "I'll see if I can't steer closer. Better to hang together rather than hang separately."

"No worries. Alpha Bravo's hanging fine."

Jay smiled. By the book. Everything by the book. If it wasn't in the book, don't even think about it. He dialed in Super Bowl I on the Holo. Green Bay Packers versus the Kansas City Chiefs. Green Bay won it 35-10, but they didn't have Jay David Buehner, BAT trooper and star player on their side. Jay decided he'd take the role of middle-linebacker this time and see if he could indirectly improve upon the score. He lost himself in the game and a chance to play on the same team as the great Bart Starr.

It felt good not to think.

"Debris field, sir!" Keri shouted it out, but knew the ship's computer would already know this, and in fact the ship had already begun evasive maneuvers. But, still regulations demanded Keri report the obvious.

"Very good, Private." The Lieutenant was also obliged to report the obvious and did so with military precision. All by the book. All totally unnecessary and yet, by regulations all very necessary.

Keri was moved by the sight of the destruction. He tried to calculate how much money he was seeing floating in space. All those ships. All that equipment. The dead men didn't cost that much, but some of those ships had at least a year's Gross Domestic Product from some smaller nations wrapped up in their production costs. Earth Central Banking would shit. He shook his head again. Milsapp's defenses were awesome. Even more awesome was the fact the planetary government had allowed Earth's government to remove the dead and injured. Earth Forces never allowed that of the enemy.

"Private, heads up. The debris field is taking out the sensors on some of our BAT troops. Eyes sharp. We'll need visual assistance for pick-up."

"Yes sir!" Keri sighed. His work actually meant something now, but he didn't think about it. He had a job to do. He did it. By the book. That was it.

Somewhere in the back of his head, Jay knew it was virtual sex. Just so many hoses and sensors connected to his body in his jump suit, but the feeling was incredible. She was Jay's favorite fantasy, a redhead with long lean legs, champagne glass breasts with a nice glowing tan, and a pair of lips he could explore for days. His sex slave was in the middle of orally pleasuring him in his favorite variation of the 69 position when he was brought out of it by the emergency klaxon on his suit. The image dissolved too quickly. He was left in a foul humor with stars exploding in his head and a rock solid hard-on when he gasped at the site in front of him.

In between his suit diversions he had set the autopilot to try to and steer closer to his BAT comrade. But, now it appeared Jay was going to have to think again. The debris field was too thick and the autopilot couldn't steer through it. Worse, a 50-foot section of a ship's bridge was headed straight for him. He could even make out a computer station and scorched, charred remnants of a bulkhead wall. He didn't want to think about what would happen if he hit that chunk of space crap at the speed he was going. He clicked on his thrusters and gave them a short micro-burst. Starboard. Aft. Starboard. He tumbled out of the way. Funny, he could hear the micro-jets inside his suit. He thought of his mother again. Wonder what she would say about that. "There's no sound in space."

Damn, idle thought got him in trouble. How could he miss that irregular portion of the deck tumbling toward him? He gave his suit full throttle. Starboard. Aft. Minus 10 degrees on the Z-axis. No Good. Again he could hear a sound. A sickening scrape, followed by a thump and a hiss. Klaxons went off. The damn deck hit him at the top of his suit. His HUD display and computer screen showed his communications array completely disabled. There went the up-link, and a minor hull breach on in the input. Sealed. No loss of coolant. Minimal atmospheric loss. He repositioned a mirror on his suit to survey the damage. Clean break. The up-link severed. His connection to the rest of humanity lost. Isolation. Loneliness. Solitude.

Fear.

Funny, he didn't know if he felt those things or just thought about them. He didn't know for sure if he felt anything.

Didn't matter. He knew his chances of retrieval now were only slightly greater than dick. Without his communications array the CAPship would have a very small chance of picking him out from all the other debris, dead suits, and space junk floating in his immediate vicinity,

He knew what the manual said. He always went by the book,

"We never leave a man behind. Do you understand that Triplett?"

"Yes, sir." Keri knew this to be true. It said so in the manual,

"Therefore, we will leave the vicinity at 1800 hours ship time whether or not we have picked up all of the remaining jump pods. Do you understand soldier?"

"Yes sir. The private understands. We never leave a man behind. We will leave *men* behind, sir."

"As you were."

It made perfect sense. The history of the Force was filled with tales of heroic rescues, horrible odds and men fighting to bring a friend home. The Force would prevail. They wouldn't leave a man behind. And if they did it was to save the entire Force. The Force was greater than any one man. It had a tradition.

Keri returned to his post and began surveying the nearby debris. So far he'd found two BAT troopers and got them home to safety. He'd find more.

He wanted to call up his mother and talk to her.

He couldn't.

He wanted to e-mail her.

He couldn't do that either.

Jay then thought of his long dead father. Well I'd have a better chance of contacting him than Mom.

"Son, all you have is yourself. Never give up that unique gift of who you are.

"Yes, Dad." What was a 9-year-old to say to his father? Especially when his father was dying?

The sedative had kicked in; he was dreaming. It would make it easier to do what he knew he must. In a hopeless situation a BAT trooper must not let his equipment fall into enemy hands. That meant the trooper couldn't fall into enemy hands either since he was part of the equipment. There was a simple and adequate solution. The small nuclear generator in his suit would, at the appropriate moment, flare with the white-hot intensity of a small sun, vaporizing the suit and anything inside it. Just dust left. But the generals on the Force were humane. Jay had to acknowledge that. They allowed you to take a sedative and then a poison that would silently, painlessly, kill you just seconds before you vaporized. It was very humane. You were even allowed to record your last will and testament or record a goodbye for your family if you wished. The up-link would send it all to the CAPship or to Central only Jay's suit was damaged and there was no one he wanted to say goodbye to anyway. His mother was too old and wouldn't understand. She never liked him joining the service anyway. And most of his girlfriends were too superficial to warrant a goodbye call to.

He looked over at the small red button on his wrist pad. He only had to open the patch, flip the switch, tongue up the medication and within 15 seconds it would be over with. By the book. He sighed. What was keeping him? Why didn't he just pull the trigger? By the book. By the book. For the Force. For humanity. For the peace loving, honor admiring Force. Only if they loved peace so much why were they always at war? And what honor was there in just offing oneself because Central didn't want your technological terror suit to fall into the hands of the enemy? Why was he thinking so damn much anyway? He knew the price of admission when he joined up. Always accepted it before. Why not now? Godamnit, what had Johnny said before the jump? He never heard Johnny talk like that before. Why now? Why just before he bought it?

He looked around, but his new orbit, brought about with his collision with the CAPship debris, had placed him out of the line of sight of any of his troopers. Right now he was in a big void of space filled with debris ranging in size from a pebble to a four-story house. He couldn't see a trooper if there was one out there anyway.

Milsapp looked nice and bright, though. For the first time, it seemed he really took notice of it. Johnny had visited his cousin there. Said it was just like Earth, without the pollution and big cities. Masturbation was legal, and you could have sex with and marry anyone you wanted. Why was simulated sex legal on earth, but not masturbation? Jay pondered that for second and then remembered the Church. That's right. In sim-sex, you didn't pleasure yourself, so it was legal. With manual masturbation you defiled yourself. Lovely logic that.

He thought again of Milsapp's planet. Johnny had said it was much freer and friendlier than Earth. Probably just a line of shit, but Johnny said it was so and Johnny wouldn't knowingly lie to Jay. His cousin said Earth's church sponsored hegemony, which Earth called missionary work, was the source of irritation between the two planets. The people on Milsapp, they just wanted to be left alone, Johnny said. Friendliest people he'd ever met. How could that be? Both friendly and standoffish. The Force wanted them in with the rest of humanity. But they wouldn't go peacefully.

It was always the backwater planets. Jay had fought at a dozen of them. Someone always had a cousin or friend on one of those backwater burgs. Most of them were horrible places, too. Super cold or super hot. Too much water or too little. The denizens always looked toothless and old - even when they were young.

Johnny said Milsapp was different. Who knew?

He fumbled with the switch on his arm. What was stopping him?

Keri looked evenly at the debris. No doubt about it now. Two more BATs unregistered on the sensors were in plain sight. One was tumbling end over end. He put the scope on it, and it came back with negative read-outs. No damage. Just a dead suit emitting it's locator beacon. Probably still in good working order, once they get rid of the deader inside. The BAT trooper probably had overdosed on Joy Juice. It happened on occasion, although the Force didn't like to let anyone know about it. The results were always the same, though. The suit would shut down, conserve energy and wait for retrieval, emitting only its emergency locator. With the suit shutdown, the trooper inside would be perfectly preserved. Upon retrieval, the Force would simply eject the human popsicle, tune up the suit and pass it on to the next trooper.

Keri shifted his attention to the other suit. It was in a more stable orbit, but something looked visibly wrong with it. Keri got it on the scope as well. Damage. The up-link, all the communication array, wiped. Thermal read-outs indicated a BAT still alive. He forwarded the information to Lieutenant Thaurus.

"Good work, Triplett." He looked over the data and turned to the Officer of the Deck. "Officer of the Deck," the Lieutenant shouted. "We have two suits sighted. BATs sir. At 42 degrees lateral, Plus .5 degrees on the Z at a quarter of a mile."

"Roger that, Lieutenant." The Officer of the Deck took the information and looked it over. "Okay helmsman, prepare to retrieve the live trooper first,"

"May I remind the Officer of the Deck that we have only 15 minutes left for retrieval. We must be underway for the next star system by then."

The Officer of the Deck looked at his helmsman. The man was right. By the book.

"Belay the order then, helmsman. Retrieve the intact suit first. If we have a chance to retrieve the BAT we will, otherwise secure the good suit."

"Aye, sir."

Jay shifted uncomfortably in his suit. He still couldn't see anything but space debris and the planet, inviting him below. There were no such things as BAT prisoners of war. A BAT flew or a BAT crashed, but the honor of the Force was maintained. He looked around again. There was still no one within sight and no way to contact the CAPship. He knew what he was supposed to do. By the book, his training taught him.

Think for yourself, his mother and father screamed at him across time.

God, he hated to have to think. A life time of Force philosophy stood against him.

"We have both pods aboard Officer of the Deck." The helmsman looked at the display. "And we are secured for light speed."

"You have permission to leave orbit."

The CAPship flared into life and began to pull away. Keri looked down at his time strip. 1600 hours. His watch was over. He sighed and smiled. Today had been a good day. He'd helped. In some small way he'd made a difference. He never felt more alive, more human. By the book. It always worked out. Always would. Wasn't it wonderful to live in a society that had already worked out all the intricacies of thought so problem solving was no problem at all?

No worries. No anxieties. Do it by the book and you were free to live your life without having to ever vex your mind. Keri was looking forward to his evening. Chow, suds, maybe a movie and some holo-games. Then sleep and up and at 'em bright and early. Great life.

Jay sighed and looked at his time strip. 1700 hours. The CAPship wasn't coming. He knew Force policy. He could no longer put off the inevitable. He was coldly, indifferently alone floating above a strange planet with no family and no friends and no one to help. He looked down at his self-destruct button.

To hell with it.

He touched the ignition on his suit and prepared for entry into Milsapp's atmosphere. Their defenses might shoot him out of the sky. He might burn up on entry. He definitely couldn't contact anyone with his uplink fried, but he had to take a chance. When he thought about it he just decided that today he didn't want to die - and this was his best chance to live. Besides, he thought to himself, if he were captured and made a prisoner, what could be so bad about a planet where masturbation was legal? He fired his thrusters and smiled. His computers told him it would take another two hours to maneuver so he could come down near the largest city.

He thought about it. Porno or John Wayne?

It was nice to be able to think.

The Hummer

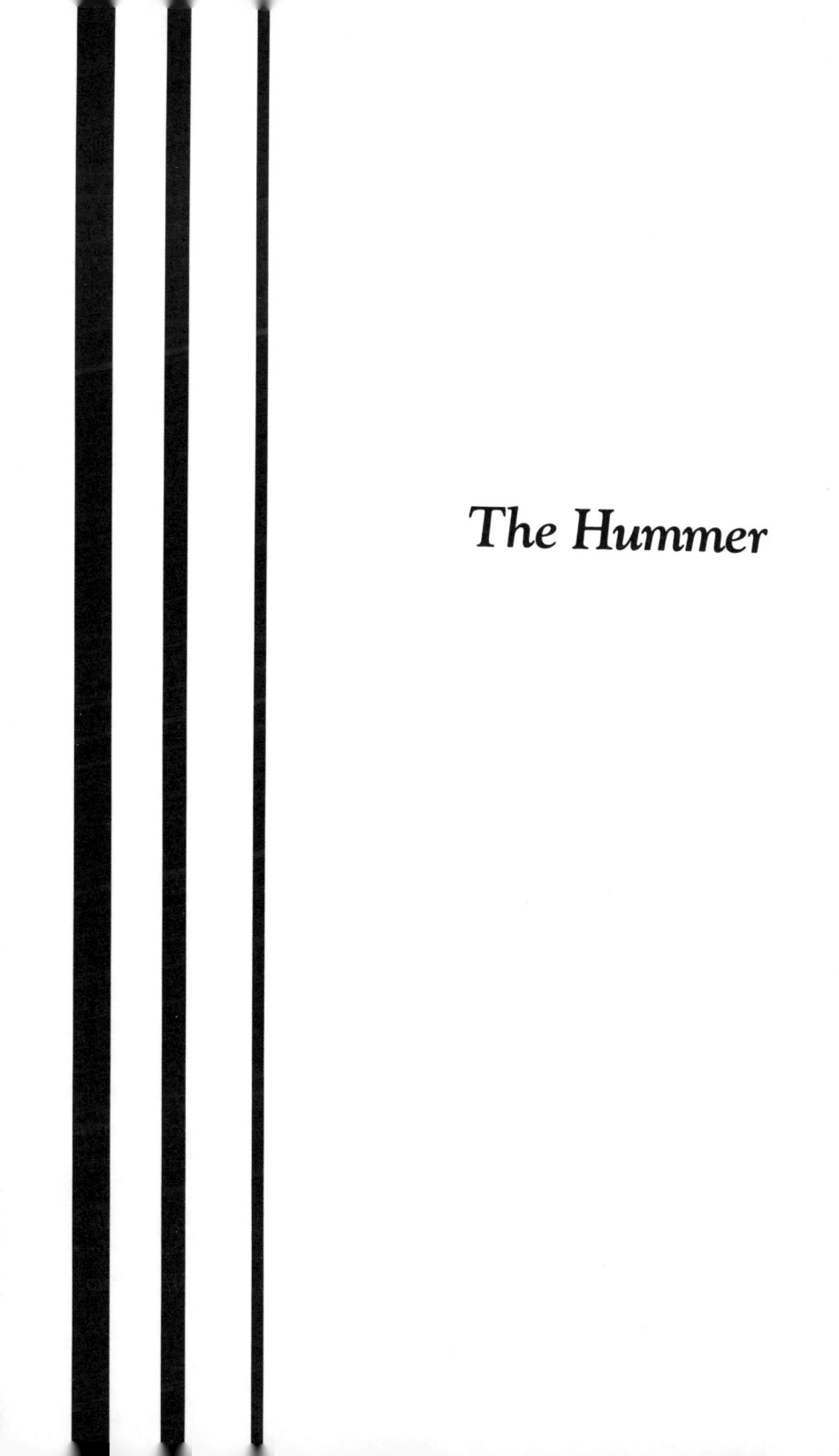

"Dear God, please don't let me have AIDS," the man said to himself as he dropped his head and folded his hands as if in prayer. "After all I've never cheated on my wife really. It was just a blow job."

"I told you you'd get AIDS you no good, fuck," his dead father said appearing over his shoulder. "You deserve it, screwing your high school teacher, screwing your sexy cousin and screwing every girl in sight. I never got to screw girls like that."

"Shut up, Dad. You always were jealous," he said out loud. Then his sexy high school teacher, the one with the big silver dollar nipple tits and tight ass, popped up over his right shoulder.

"You know you're pretty safe. It was just a blow job. It wasn't as good a blow job as I give, but you can't get AIDS from a blow job, honey." She blew him a kiss, but from his left shoulder he heard his father shout.

"You can too get AIDS from a blow job!"

"You're crazy," his teacher told his father as she began to pull off her clothes and masturbate. "You can't catch AIDS from saliva. So as long as you only kissed her and got a blow job, he can't get AIDS." She shook her vibrator as she lectured his father.

"It would serve him right to get AIDS," his father countered. "He's got his second child on the way and he deserves to catch AIDS."

His father was about to jump at the teacher when the man put down his marijuana cigarette. "I gotta stop smoking this shit. It's gonna kill me," he said and leafed his sinewy fingers through his thick, reddish brown hair. "God, I better not have AIDS."

"Can I help you now, sir?" the waitress asked rather reluctantly.

She was back at his table. His thoughts had been awash in smoldering images of a fiery afterlife when she spoke.

He glanced around. Shit. He'd been talking to himself at this stupid diner. No wonder the waitress stared at him so strangely. "What? Oh, I'm sorry. I was thinking about something."

"Uh, huh. I heard. You okay honey? You look rather pale."

"No. I'm fine." He said with a sickly smile. How much had she heard? What had he said out loud? Christ.

"Well, I'd put that away if I were you," she said nodding at the cigarette. "Since we're an all night place we get a lot of cops in here. Seems silly to get busted for a roach." He looked down at the marijuana. Had he forgotten he was in a public place? Jesus, people could recognize him. A county magistrate couldn't be caught smoking a hummer in a public place. It could ruin his life.

"Sorry," he mumbled as he put the roach out in his hand and then dropped it into his coat pocket. "Just bring me a cup of coffee."

She smiled. In an earthy kind of way, even without two of her teeth she looked kind of cute. "Right away, honey." As she walked off he couldn't help but notice the twitch in her stride, the long, lean legs, the full breasts and her slim figure.

"God, I'm a slave to my penis," he thought. "I'm a no good, shallow, perspiring slave to slam-me-down on the ground, lick-me-up-and-down sex. I'm gonna catch AIDS. I'm gonna die at the age of 40. I'm a wisp, a pale shadow of my former self. I'm a whore." He took the dull butter knife from the table and set about, in a rather determined fashion, to slash his wrist. But the butter knife, being what it was – dull, and he being what he was – stoned, he didn't make much progress.

He was thinking of writing Dear Abby or the Surgeon General when a young, tan woman in a tight sweater and blue jeans walked up to him. He barely noticed, being stoned and intent on cutting his wrist.

"Are you attempting suicide, or is that just a little suicidal gesture?" she said in a think Jersey accent. It didn't sound like a question.

"I'm sorry," he said. He looked up, startled, into the greenest eyes he'd ever seen. "You caught me at a rather bad time. I'm having a hell of a day."

"I can see that. Maybe I can help."

"You a therapist?"

"No. This isn't The Sopranos."

"Hey, I'm no mobster either," he said.

"With that color hair, no. I didn't think so." She reached her hand across the table and embraced his. With her free hand she ran it through his hair. He smiled. Her hand was smooth and soft. Her face was gifted in its beauty and her breasts, he thought, would fill out a champagne glass rather nicely. All thoughts of suicide disappeared.

"Check please," he said to the waitress who rolled her eyes and brought it over.

"How can you help?" he said to the green-eyed woman as he put a five dollar bill down on the counter.

"I've always been a sucker for a charity case," she said.

"Great," he smiled and stood up. She grabbed him and kissed him passionately.

He left a happy man.

Just Before the Five Families War

"REMEMBER THAT SCENE IN GOODFELLAS?"
"What? The one where he's talking about being a clown?"
"No."
"What, the one where the guy says everything twice, like he wants to get a paper, get a paper?"
"No. I think that's the same scene. I mean the very first scene where the guys are drivin' with Billy Batts in the trunk of the car and you think they like ran over somethin' and then they get out of the car and then there's this freeze frame and the one guy says . . ."
"You mean Joe Pesci?"
"No, the other guy."
"Who? Bobby D?"
"No. The other, other guy. Ray uh. . ."
"Yeah, yeah. Him. He was in *Copland*, too."
"There was a *Copland Two*?"
"No, I mean he was also in *Copland*. He was banging Lorraine Bracco in *GoodFellas*."
"Now that broad had a nice ass. Great legs too."
"You know who was real good in that movie?"
"Who?"
"Paul Sorvino."
"Now there's a guy with a good looking daughter."
"Did you see him crying at the Oscars with her? Jesus, that's a good father."
"Yeah, I'd love to fuck his daughter."
"'Henry ,you gonna help me fuck this Jew broad or what?'"

"Fuckin' morons. Bust a place out and sit there while it's burning. That's fuckin' stupid."

"Remember, though, he always wanted to be a gangster! Ha!"

"Yeah. That's what I was talking about. In that first scene. The big freeze frame with the trunk lid up and that actor Ray, the one who was banging Lorraine Bracco, says he always wanted to be a gangster."

"Yeah, so what's your point?"

"I always wanted to be a spy."

"A spy? What the fuck did you want to be a spy for?"

"You know, James Bond. Action and adventure and banging bitches with names like 'Pussy Galore'."

"Those were fuckin' great names. That fuckin' Austin Powers movie"

"Piece of shit."

"Exactly. Fuckin' take that Mike Myers and bitch slap him like the little faggot he is."

"What about Heather, uh, what's her name in that movie. The blonde in the second one?"

"Oh, yeah, I think she was Roller Girl in *Boogie Nights*"

"Another piece of shit movie."

"Except for Burt Reynolds."

"Yeah. He was good. 'Okay, fuck her in the ass.'"

"You know Joey's girl, that one on the side?"

"Yeah, she's a niece piece."

"Tommy. She takes it up the ass."

"Get the fuck outta here. Really?"

"Joey told me himself. Said the bitch likes it."

"Mikey, I knew there was a reason I liked that broad."

"Yeah, you know who else takes it up the ass?"

"Who?"

"Remember that broad in *Airport*. The stewardess that Dean Martin was bangin'?"

"Man, I miss Dino. He was the coolest member of the Rat Pack."

"How did they ever get hooked up with Joey Bishop?"

"I heard Dino and Frankie used to give him their leftovers."

"Just like a Jew."

"So, anyway, what's the deal with the broad in *Airport*?"

"Oh, yeah, I heard Nick Nolte fucked her in the ass."

"Really? Where did you hear that? In your fuckin' dreams?"

"No. Carlie's cousin, Jimmy. He works in the union out on the coast. Builds sets and shit. Ended up a drunk and in the program with Nolte. Said one night Nolte showed up in his slippers and bathrobe. Jimmy was wearin' the same shit, so they kind of hit it off. Jimmy says Nolte's been fuckin' a steady train of broads for years."

"Now that's a train I want on."

"Yeah, and you want to be a spy, too."

"What's that supposed to mean?"

"It sounds like you wanna be a rat."

"Fuck you, Mikey. I ain't no rat. I'm talking about undercover and flying helicopters and banging broads in the ass. You know, spy shit."

"Tommy, you start talking about 'undercover' and that sounds like subversive shit. Real Henry Hill crap."

"Get the fuck out of here. Mikey, I'm talking about a fuckin' movie."

"You know Joey Doves?"

"That guy with the crew in Jersey?"

"Yeah."

"No, I don't know him."

"He went over to the other side."

"He went to Naples?"

"No, you fuckin' moron. Went to the Feds. Got a mess of guys popped. He was a 'spy'."

"Mikey, you better fuckin' take that back. I ain't no fuckin' rat."

"I'm just sayin'. You know, like in *GF2*."

"They made a second *GoodFellas*?"

"No. You fuckin' idiot. The Godfather. The second one. His own brother was the rat."

"You got fuckin' rats on the brain. I'm surprised you don't have one gnawin' at your fuckin' medusa oblongata."

"What the fuck is that?"

"It's part of your fuckin' brain you fuckin' idiot."

"Always the big words. I think you're upset because I called you a rat."

"No shit. That's exactly why I'm upset."

"You wouldn't be upset unless you got somethin' to hide. You a rat Tommy?"

"Mikey, I ain't shittin'. You'd better take that back-"

"Or what tough guy? What are you gonna fuckin' do?"

"Hey, Lou?"
"Yeah, what is it Henry?"
"Dispatch called. Looks like a couple of wise guys capped each other at an outdoor diner down on Mulberry."
"Fuck. I haven't heard anything about a war. Isn't detective Harris supposed to be-"
"Whoa. Relax Lou. Waitress said they just got into an argument over some movies."
"You sure? No war? It sounds kind of thin that a couple of wiseguys would kill each other over a movie. Who were they?"
"Tommy Caggiano and Mikey Patrullo."
"Okay check with the FBI Task Force. That name Patrullo rings a bell for some reason. Caggiano, he's a made guy isn't he?"
"From what the guys in the squad tell me they both were. But they were nothin' more than soldiers."
"Anyways, check with the Task Force."
"You got it Lou."

"Jake get the phone. Jake . . . Jake! Shit. Never mind . . . Task Force, Detective James speaking."
"This is Henderson at the 11th precinct. You Bobby James?"
"Yeah. What's going on?"
"We got two dead wiseguys at a diner on Mulberry. Wondering if you knew 'em."
"Who are they?"
"One is a guy by the name of Tommy Caggiano and the other is a guy by the name of Patrullo. Uh, Mikey, I think."
"Shit. Yeah. I knew them. Runnin' buddies. Caggiano is a real moron. Who killed them?"
"Looks like they killed each other. Waitress says they was arguin' about movies."
"No. That ain't right. Mikey, that bald fuck, worked with us a little bit. Real paranoid. Thought everybody was on to him. He might have been right. Shit."
"Well, look I talked to the waitress-"
"Fuck that. I'll be down in about five minutes. Where did you say

it was?"

"Dave. Dave, can you hear me?"
"I can hear you, Beth. It's a cell phone, not a megaphone. What?"
"You gotta do a live shot at the top of the six o'clock news."
"What on? This fuckin' zoo story is a bust. There aren't any missing chimps. Turned out they were just hiding in the underbrush. The zoo keeper got all bent out of shape and figured the guys who broke in last night stole the-"
"No, no. We're sending you over to Little Italy. A couple of Mafia guys killed each other. It's like some big gang war or something is going on."
"Shit. Okay. Gimme directions."

". . . But first, at the top of the news this evening, a bloody gang war has apparently broken out in Little Italy. Police and FBI agents say two well-known mobsters were dining at Ginzo's on Mulberry when their discussion erupted in gunfire. Police and FBI agents at this hour are unsure of the motive behind the gangland slaying but sources tell us the New York Mob may be headed toward the bloodiest war in years. Here with the exclusive on the bloody gangland massacre is Dave Tarr . . ."

That's Harry, Son

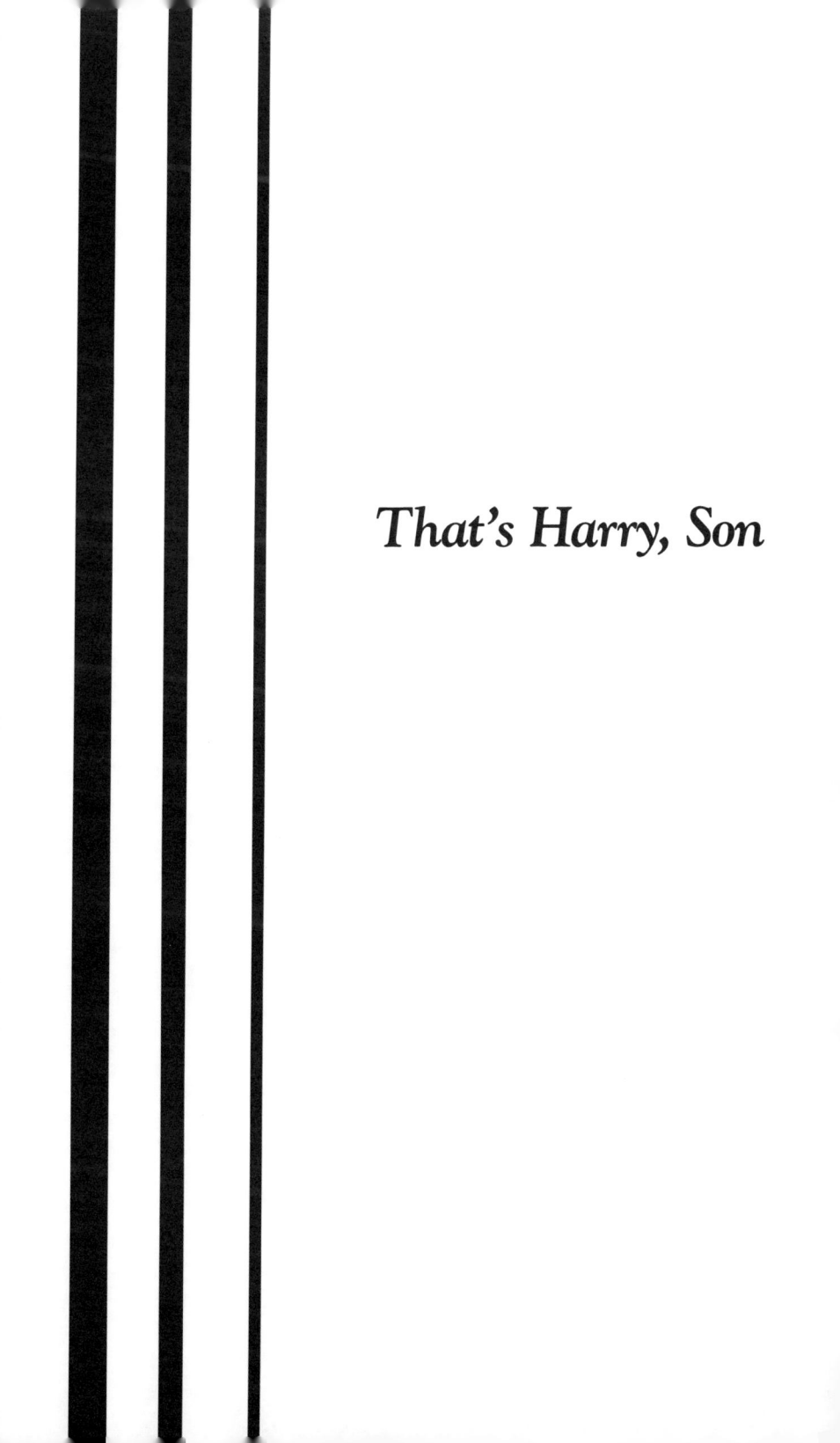

"YES, OF COURSE I KILLED HIM. I killed him quickly. Killed, murdered, exterminated, squelched, quashed, slayed, slaughtered, put to the sword, destroyed, butchered, did in, liquidated, smote, struck him dead, cut him down, massacred, bumped him off, took him for a ride, punched his ticket, fed him to the fishes, gave him cement overshoes. For God's sake, I snuffed him out." The man was a whimpering piece of jello. He sweat continuously and slithered in his own turgid body slime.

The police officer ground out his cigar in his sandpaper palm, turned to the man in the chair, grabbed him, and held him up to the bare 150 - watt light bulb hanging down from the ceiling. He slowly pressed the man's cheek into the searing heat of the lamp. He could smell sweat and flesh sizzle.

"Quit beating around the bush. Did you have anything to do with the death of Hector Pinta-Santa Maria?"

"For the last goddamn time. I wiped him out. I murdered him. I cut his life short. I took a .44 Magnum to his head and pulled the trigger. I splashed his brains all over the concrete. I danced in his blood and cut his life short."

"Shit." The cop threw the man back to the chair.

"You're not going to get anything from this scum. He's one tough customer," said the cop's partner.

"You're right, Detective Blastocyst, but I still can't help but think this slug had something to do with this Santa Maria character's death."

"I did it, goddamnit, I did it," the man was now shouting from the chair.

"Shut up you common street scum." The cop backslapped him.

"Sgt. Morosis do you think you should hit him? He may be innocent."

"Goddamnit, you ignorant pigs, I'm not innocent. Are you deaf? I told you cum-guzzling gutter sluts that I DID IT! The man was fooling around with my wife, and I blew him away. I stuck him. I creamed him. I made him cannon fodder. I made him meet his maker. I blew him into next week. I did him. I offed him. I killed THE SON OF A BITCH!"

Sgt. Morosis slapped him again. "Mind your manners you, or I'll have you up on charges so fast it'll make your head swim." He then turned to detective Blastocyst. "I normally don't agree with violence, but sometimes you have to make an exception with street stench." Morosis took a deep breath and smoothed his wrinkled white shirt over his pudgy belly and then stuffed the shirt in his pleated pants. Then he took another deep breath, wiped stray cigar ashes from his shirt, lit another El Producto cigar and sat down. His short, stubby fingers ran themselves through his equally short, stubby grey hair. He huffed, he puffed and then put his feet up on a file cabinet, permanently dented from repeated attempts by Morosis to rest his bulky feet there.

Meanwhile the slim, younger Detective Blastocyst leaned against another filing cabinet, loosened his tie, and took his hat off. He meticulously put it in the top drawer of another file cabinet, then tried to relax. He glanced over at Morosis and saw the chunky sergeant taking in deep, gallon-sized breaths. For perhaps the millionth time he wondered why the man always wore white socks and black shoes. Didn't he know that was not being style conscious?

"I suppose you think we're really stupid, Mr. Matar, that we'd believe this supercilious story of puerile salaciousness."

"God, yes. You've finally gotten something right. I do think you're stupid. Incredibly, unbelievably ignorant and stupid."

"All right smart mouth, I warned you." And again he slapped him down. "If you don't watch yourself I'll put you away for a long, long time. Now, what do you know about Mr. Pinta-Santa Maria's death and when did you know it?"

"You stupid pig," the man laughed. "All right. I give up. I don't have any idea who killed this Pointed Marina guy."

Sgt. Morosis was about to slap him again, but changed his mind.

"That's better you verbose dung heap. Now get out of this office and don't try anything else stupid. And if you ever decide to turn to crime don't forget that Sgt. Morosis is out there waiting for you." And then he did slap the man. "Now get lost."

The man eagerly left the office, and Sgt. Morosis leaned even further back in his chair.

"Detective Blastocyst, go down the street and get me a piece of toast and a large strawberry malted. This has been a rough case."

"Gee, okay, Sgt. Morosis."

The sergeant looked fondly upon the youth. He was catching on quick. "Call me Harry, son."

"Okay, Harry, son. I didn't know you were Japanese."

"What?" But by that time Blastocyst had already left.

Who Forgot to Duck

MY FIRST RECOLLECTION of my younger brother dates from his third day of life. My mother had just got home from the hospital, and she placed his crib next to the wall in the living room directly across from the old black and white television set that had been our link to the world for the last few days as we watched Walter Cronkite tell us about John F. Kennedy, Lee Harvey Oswald, Lyndon Johnson, Dallas, book depositories, assassinations, rifles, and other things that were to be forever bludgeoned into my memory.

My younger brother remained blissfully unaware that he'd picked such an historical time to enter the world. My father claims his timing has been screwed ever since. Nonetheless, there he sat. While we watched television, my mother cried, my dad cussed, I looked bewildered, and my younger brother just gurgled and cooed. Somewhere during that time my father, in his green, plaid Bermuda shorts, escaped with the newspaper to make one of his hour long forays into his library - the bathroom to everyone else.

He'd been gone for just a few minutes into his hour-long marathon when my mother and I heard a gastric eruption of biblical proportions coming from my brother's crib. Mom, in her white cotton shirt, Laura Petrie slacks, and Jackie Kennedy hairdo got up and ventured a cautious glance into the crib. I followed. My nose told me the story before my eyes could sort out the damage. My brother had deposited the remains of his latest liquid nourishment into his cloth diaper in the form of a gelatinous solid. Unfortunately, the volume of his deposit far exceeded the volume able to be safely controlled by the diaper. As a result, rich, brown excrement now filled the lower half of the crib.

"Ted, come here right now! The baby pooped all over the crib!" My mother shouted in her best "Oh, Rob," Laura Petrie voice.

"What the hell do you want me to do woman?" boomed my father's baritone from his ceramic tiled library. He then finished his loud verbal beating of my mother with, "Can't you see I'm still on the toilet," foreshadowing Archie Bunker by eight years.

By the time he was three-years-old my brother had acquired a taste for the eclectic tunes of his favorite Disney characters and an assortment of Mother Goose nursery rhymes. Grimm's fairy-tales were far too grim for him, but "Whistle While you Work", "The Sorcerer's Apprentice," and "The Three Little Pigs" received almost unending airplay on my brother's small white-plastic, portable record player. One Sunday, alas, the needle broke on his favorite toy. Ears throughout our household sighed with relief, until my brother's high pitched screams brought my mother, father and half of the neighborhood dogs running to him.

"What's wrong?" my parents shouted in unison.

When they found out my brother's tale of woe, my father reluctantly, with a small smile on his sad face, told my brother he could no longer play his favorite record player, and since it was a Sunday, no needle could be purchased to fix the record player until the following morning. Undaunted, my brother sneaked out of the house, threw his record player into my father's powder-blue Valiant station wagon and kicked the car out of gear and into neutral.

Since the car rested on an incline in our driveway, the laws of physics dictated that the car must now roll backward down the hill-which of course it did.

My mother's screams brought me running to see this, as they did my father, who had cut short another trip to his favorite library. I rushed to the front door in time to see my brother's little brown-haired head bouncing up and down just barely over the top of the dashboard on the driver's seat. He was shouting "I want my record player fixed! I want my record player fixed!"

Frozen in my mind is the image of my mom's white, slender thighs escaping the confines of her blue flannel robe as she hurdled over the hedges that lined the front sidewalk. Coming up from behind, and then passing her, was my father. First pulling up his boxer shorts, then sucking heavily at an unfiltered cigarette that clung to his mouth, he reached the car and managed to stop it before anyone suffered any serious injury.

By the time my brother was five he'd been diagnosed as being hyperactive. Some doctors thought he was retarded, some thought he was dyslexic; one actually checked him for a brain tumor- he had none. But he did have a knack for getting himself into situations that seemed to turn my mother's hair gray and cause my father to spend far less time reading and smoking cigarettes in his library than he wanted.

One time my brother painted his face multi-colors with the oil paints from a paint-by-numbers kit and proudly marched around the neighborhood announcing that he was a "little colored boy." The African-American family that lived three doors down in a nice, middle-class brick house laughed the hardest at my brother's charade. It turned out that their son and my brother were playmates and my brother enjoyed his friend's color more than his own, and hence the performance art.

My brother also marched into the kitchen one morning as my mom sat drinking coffee and reading the newspaper. I watched as he walked up behind her, grabbed about six inches of her flowing, blonde hair and then, with a pair of scissors, he hacked it all off. "Mean old Mom," he said as he cut her hair. Turns out he was upset that he was told to clean up his room.

My mother's resounding screams are probably still being heard somewhere in the galaxy.

Shortly after my brother turned six-years-old, my father purchased a pair of electric clippers. It was his grand idea to cut our hair in order to save money on haircuts. By this time I'd begun fighting with my father over the length of my hair. If the Beatles could wear their hair long, then I was determined to as well. My brother, however, had no such hippie yearnings. In fact, he liked hair cuts so much, that after my father cut his hair one Saturday morning, my brother grabbed the shears later that same afternoon and shaved off every bit of his hair- even his eyebrows.

There was little my parents could do.

The following day, Sunday, my brother ran away from home.

For some reason, which escapes me now, my father decided to go to church alone that morning. My brother wanted to go with him, and, in fact, my mother thought he had. However, when my father returned from church, my mother learned, to her horror, that my brother had disappeared. Naturally, panic set it. My parents called the police. My sisters cried. We hopped in the car and drove around the neighborhood looking for my brother. My sisters cried. We stopped the car. My father threatened my sisters. My sisters cried. Finally, a young woman pulled her car next to ours.

"Are you looking for a little lost boy?" she asked.
"Yes," my mother shouted. "Yes."
"Is his name Henry?"
"Henry?" My mom was stunned. "No it's not."
"Well, maybe we didn't understand him correctly. You want to see if it's your little boy."
"Yes. Dear, God, yes!" came my mother's melodramatic reply.

My father dutifully drove to the awaiting domicile, which turned out to be right around the corner from our house. As we pulled up to the house, my brother walked out of the front door of the home, a Hostess Twinkie in one hand and a glass of milk in the other.

"Hi, Mom!" He shouted.

"Hey, he has a Twinkie. I want a Twinkie. How come he gets a Twinkie?" my sisters shouted from the back of the car. After a withering stare from my father, the girls quieted down and my brother got into the car.

My mother was relieved and my father dismayed. How in the name of GOD, my father wanted to know, could my little brother give the name of Henry to the people who'd been so kind as to take in such an obviously malnourished and disheveled runaway? It turns out that my brother, thinking he would get in trouble if his parents found out he ran away, gave a false name to his rescuers - just to be safe. Since he had a bald head from his previous day with my father's hair clippers, he thought it would be best to give the name of the little bald kid that appeared in the comic section of the newspaper.

As it turns out, my brother had more than a passing infatuation with comics and comic books. When the Charlie Brown movie came out in the early 70s, my brother conned my mother into seeing the movie at least three times. She became so flabbergasted at my brother's continuing interest in this film, she finally found it necessary to purchase a long play record and comic book that told the same story as the movie. It wasn't long before my brother was running around the house quoting huge chunks of memorized dialogue.

"Owning ten-percent of Charlie Brown is like owning ten percent of nothing!" he declared one morning when told he had to go to school. He casually told his teacher his new name was Linus Van Pelt, and he and his sister Lucy, the teacher was informed, were going to own an ink factory.

When I was 15-years-old my parents had been divorced for about two years, and I took my nine-year-old kid brother with me one night on a joy ride in my mother's 1970 Chevy Impala. In Louisville, Kentucky fireworks, you see, were illegal then. But, some 200 miles down the road, in Nashville, Tennessee, they were legal. So, together we got up a bunch of orders from neighbor kids, and after charging a 20 percent commission, I figured we'd make quite a bundle.

So, I had no license. So I was too young to drive. So, I didn't own a car. My mother went to bed early. I figured a three hour ride down. We get there a little after midnight, and get back a couple of hours before my mother woke in the morning.

It was a perfect plan.

We got down there, found an all night fireworks stand, purchased the fireworks and got back- almost.

About 30 miles from home a good-ole-boy sheriff's deputy pulled us over because we had a taillight out. I knew I was in trouble when he asked me for my driver's license.

"I don't have one sir."

"Boy. How old are you?" He said as he scrutinized my face.

"Uh, fifteen, sir."

"Boy don't you know you got to be 16-years-old to operate a motor vehicle in the state of Kentucky?"

"Why, no, sir, I didn't." I said, hoping to find a way out of the mess. Of course, I didn't find a way out. We were arrested and hauled into the sheriff's office where we spent the night.

I cried.

My brother didn't.

A year after this famed incident, I managed to get my driver's license and so, with my new found freedom I didn't spend as much time with my brother any more. I had girls to impress, guys to hang out with, and cruising to be done. To augment my freedom I took a part-time job at a fast food restaurant and with the money I purchased an AMC Gremlin - you remember, one of those little hatchbacks that looked as if someone had cutoff the rear-half of the car. The car was canary yellow and as ugly to look at as it was to drive. But, it got me around. Well for a while anyway. One day the fuel pump burst, and I had to have my chariot fixed. I moaned, I groaned, and I finally gave into my car's demands. It sat in a shop for a day. And on that day I found I'd once more have to ride the school bus.

Naturally, I sat next to my little brother. He seemed thrilled and we talked of baseball for a few minutes, until a kid I didn't know began picking on my little brother. First, he called him retarded. Then he called him a scaredy-cat, then he called him a faggot. My brother was 10 years old. His tormentor, as it turned out, was 15-years-old and about my size. The match-up hardly seemed fair.

"Leave him alone," I told the bully.

"Who are you? His protector?"

"I'm his brother, you asshole. He hasn't done anything to you. We're minding our own business. So, why don't you mind yours."

The bully replied, loudly enough for the whole bus to hear that my brother was "a pussy" for having me on the bus to protect him. He also stated, in very blunt terms, that I had been called in by my brother on purpose, to protect him.

The bus was pulling up to my stop by then. I rose, as did my little brother, who was very clearly afraid. I took him by the hand and marched toward the front of the bus, where my brother's tormentor still stood flapping his lips. In one quick motion, I grabbed the bully and heaved him off the bus. I was ready to engage in the manly art of fisticuffs in order to defend my little brother. But, it turned out the tormentor had no stomach for physical violence, so he ran away. The other kids on the bus laughed, and I looked down to see my brother smiling through tear-stained eyes. We talked more of baseball on the block walk home and the episode was forgotten. A friend of mine came over about a half an hour later, and the three of us decided we'd take the rest of the afternoon and go to a nearby pond and go fishing.

As we sat discussing these plans in our open garage, I heard a car pull up. My brother's face froze, and then he opened the door to the house and ran inside. I turned and looked and saw ten kids pile out of not one, but two cars. Most of the kids were about my age, but one of them was 18-years-old, much larger than I was, and quite mean as it turned out.

"You kicked Ben's ass," he told me, pointing to the kid I'd heaved off the school bus for making fun of my brother. "Now we're going to kick your ass." The ten of them fanned out in my drive-way. I turned and looked at my friend, who turned and looked at me. He was armed with a fishing pole. I picked up my Al Kaline model 33 Louisville Slugger. I'd be damned if I was going to take an ass-whipping in my own backyard.

"Okay," I said, "the first idiot that steps forward is going to get smacked with this bat."

"I'm not afraid," the nearest lint-head stooge said. He promptly stepped forward. Just as quickly, I took a home run swing at his ribs. I heard them crack as he fell into a heap. Through a raspy voice, he then asked one of his buddies for help.

They hauled him off and, thinking I was crazy, I suppose, the rest of the guys piled into the cars and took off.

After I got married I saw less and less of my brother, although we stayed close and talked to each other by telephone. He had a hard time in college, a rough time with women, and couldn't find a job. Finally, out of desperation, he joined the Army as a Second Lieutenant. He found himself, he swore, serving Uncle Sam.

"You don't understand, bro'," I remember him telling me. "You never served. But I'm in charge of people here. They respect me. I'm nobody's little brother-"

"Hey, that's not fair," I said.

"No. You don't understand. I don't mean you've done anything wrong, okay? But, I'm my own person here. And, I have friends. People accept me and respect me." He said that twice- "respect me."

"Well, okay. If you're happy that's what matters."

"Thanks bro'. It means a lot to me that you approve."

"Well, brother," I told him. "It means a lot to me that you're happy." I remember the day he called me up and told me he was going to be stationed in Germany.

"I'm going over seas bro', can you believe it?"

"I'm really happy for you man. That's great."

"There is a God! Yes!"

I thought it was kind of silly, my brother defending our country. But, he never seemed happier. His life was going in the right direction.

Naturally, when the Persian Gulf War broke out, he went.

"Don't worry bro'," he said. "We'll kick Saddam's ass and be home in time for Christmas." My mother called me yesterday. More than one hundred soldiers were killed in their barracks at the airbase in Dhahran, Saudi Arabia after Saddam launched a scud missile at the city.

My brother was one of them.

About the Author

Former President George Bush called him "rude." Former Speaker of the House Newt Gingrich refused to be interviewed by him saying, "I'd rather talk to anyone else." And syndicated columnist Carl Rowan once said that he wished ". . . we had a hundred reporters with the guts and irreverence that [Karem] displayed.

Brian Karem is an award-winning investigative reporter, writer, producer, and former correspondent for *America's Most Wanted*. Mr. Karem's extensive work as a reporter has taken him around the world. He was the first American reporter allowed inside Pablo Escobar's palatial prison after Escobar's escape from Columbian authorities, and he was one of the first reporters to enter Kuwait City after its liberation during the Gulf War.

Shield the Source (New Horizon Press, 1992) chronicles the events when Mr. Karem was jailed for protecting a confidential source. He was presented with the National Press Club's Freedom of the Press Award. Mr. Karem is also the author of *Above the Law* (Pinnacle Books, 1999) and *Innocent Victims* (2000). A regular contributor to *People* magazine, Mr. Karem has also interviewed James Carville, Mary Matalin, and G. Gordon Liddy for *Playboy*.

Mr. Karem lives outside of Washington, D. C., near Gaithersburg, Maryland, with his wife, Pamela, and his children, Zachary, Brennan, and Wyatt.